ISBN: 979-8-3291-1124-8

Table of Contents

Introduction

What is Vue.js?

Vue.js is a super popular JavaScript framework for building user interfaces. That last part is really important – Vue's main focus is on building user interfaces (UIs) and it does that really well! Vue doesn't try to do too much. It doesn't focus on other things like routing or making requests to the server.

But what about all those other things you need to build a web app? Don't worry! Vue has a huge ecosystem of other powerful libraries that you can add to your project. You've got Vuex for complex state management, Vue Router for handling navigation between pages, andBootstrap Vue for nice looking UI elements. There are tons of libraries out there, so you'll have no trouble finding what you need.

Why Learn Vue.js?

Here's the deal: Vue currently has over 175,000 stars on its GitHub repository. That makes it one of the most popular open-source projects in the world. Does that mean it's better than React or other frameworks? Not necessarily. It just means that a lot of developers around the world love using it!

Because it has such a large community, you're going to find answers to almost any problem you encounter. That's a huge advantage! It's always nice to know that you can find help online when you're stuck.

But let's talk about the technical reasons why Vue is so awesome. The Vue docs list three main benefits:

- **Vue is Approachable:** Getting started with Vue is incredibly easy. All you need is a basic understanding of HTML, CSS, and JavaScript. You can even add a script tag to your webpage, link it to the Vue.js library, and start building right away! Vue also has some really helpful tools to make development a breeze, like Vue Devtools for inspecting your apps and Vue CLI for quickly creating and managing your projects. It also uses a component-based architecture, which lets you break down your application into smaller, reusable pieces. This makes your code much easier to manage and helps prevent errors.

- **Vue is Versatile:** You have the choice! You can use Vue to build super powerful single-page applications (SPAs) from scratch using build tools like Webpack. Or, you can easily add Vue to your existing websites for progressive enhancements. This means you can start using Vue in small parts of your website without needing to rewrite the entire thing.

- **Vue is Performant:** Vue is super lightweight, only about 20 kilobytes when compressed. It also uses a technique called the "virtual DOM," which only updates the parts of your web page that have changed. This means your web apps run fast and smooth!

Vue really is a fantastic framework. It takes the best parts from other libraries and frameworks, and it does everything just a little bit better! If you're familiar with React, you'll actually find a lot of similarities.

Prerequisites for Learning Vue

As I mentioned, you'll need a good understanding of HTML, CSS, and JavaScript to get the most out of this series. We'll also be using some of the newer features of JavaScript, so make sure you're familiar with ES6 and beyond.

Don't worry, you don't need to be an expert! Just knowing the basics will be enough. But there are a few concepts that will make it much easier to write Vue code. You can get my book on Javascript.

My goal is to help everyone, from complete beginners to those with some experience, become Vue experts.

It's time to dive in and create our first "Hello World" application. We'll be doing that in the next section!

Let's Get Started!

Let's get our hands dirty and create our very first Vue application!

First things first, we need to set up our development environment. Think of it like preparing your tools for a big project. We need two main things:

- **Node.js:** Node.js is a JavaScript runtime environment, which basically means it allows you to run JavaScript code outside of a web browser.

We'll need this to work with Vue. Head over to nodejs.org and download the latest stable version. If you already have Node.js installed, make sure you update it to the latest version.

- **Text Editor:** We need a text editor to write our code. I recommend VS Code. It's free, super popular, and has excellent support for Vue.js. You can download and install VS Code from code.visualstudio.com.

Once you have VS Code installed, open it up and install the "Vuter" or "Vue - Official" extension. This extension is like a superpower for your VS Code, giving you cool features for working with Vue.js. You'll find the extensions tab on the left-hand side of VS Code. Search for "Vuter" or "Vue" and install either Vuter or Vue - Official.

Now, let's create a folder called "vue.js3" and open it in VS Code. This folder will be our workspace for the rest of our projects.

Choosing the Right Path: Vue Project Setup

There are four main ways to add Vue to a project. We'll focus on one specific approach, but it's good to know your options:

- **CDN (Content Delivery Network):** You can include Vue as a CDN package. Think of it like borrowing tools from a big library. All you need to do is add a `<script>` tag to your HTML file. If you've worked with jQuery before, this will feel familiar. This is a good option for small projects or if you want to quickly add Vue to an existing website.

- **NPM (Node Package Manager):** This is the preferred approach when you're building larger applications with Vue. Inside your project folder, you'll run the command `npm install vue` and Vue 3 will be installed. It's a bit more involved than the CDN method, but gives you more control over your project.

- **Vue CLI (Command Line Interface):** The official Vue CLI is super helpful for scaffolding single-page applications. It's like having a magic wand that sets up a complete Vue project with a few simple commands. You'd run `npm install -g @vue/cli` and then `vue create [project name]`. This method is great for beginners because it takes care of a lot of the setup for you.

- **Vite:** Vite is a modern build tool for web development. It uses ES modules, which makes everything faster and smoother. It's similar to the Vue CLI, but with a simpler setup and even faster development experience. To set up a Vue project with Vite, you'd run `npm init vite@latest [project name]`.

For this series, we'll be using the **Vue CLI**. It's a solid choice for beginners and allows us to focus on understanding the concepts of Vue without getting bogged down in complex configuration files.

Our First Vue Application

Let's get this party started! Open your command prompt (or terminal) and run it as administrator. This is important so that Vue gets added to your system's environment variables.

Inside the command prompt, navigate to your "vue.js3" folder. Then run the following command:

```
yarn global add @vue/cli
```

If you prefer npm, use the command:

```
npm install -g @vue/cli
```

This will install the Vue CLI globally on your system. It might take a few seconds. Once it's done, run:

```
vue --version
```

This will tell you the version of the Vue CLI you have installed.

Now, we're ready to create our project! In the command prompt, run:

```
vue create hello-world
```

You'll be asked if you want to switch your npm registry. Choose "no".

Next, you'll be presented with some presets for your project. We'll choose the **default** preset for our simple "hello-world" application. This preset includes Babel and ESLint, which help you write better and cleaner code. You can also choose your package manager (npm or yarn).

The command will take some time to run. Once it's done, you'll have a new folder called "hello-world" in your "vue.js3" folder.

Running Your Vue Application

Open VS Code and navigate to the "hello-world" folder. Now, open your terminal inside VS Code (you can find it under "View" > "Terminal").

Inside the terminal, run:

```
yarn serve
```

or if you're using npm:

```
npm run serve
```

This command will start a development server on your local machine (usually at `http://localhost:8080`). Click the link in the terminal, and your browser will open to your brand new Vue application!

You'll see a simple page with a few links that guide you through getting started.

Congratulations! You've just created your first Vue application.

Project Structure

We learned how to create and run a basic Vue application using the Vue CLI. Now, it's important to understand the files and folders that make up our project. Let's take a deep dive!

Open our Hello World project in VS Code, and you'll see three folders and five files at the root level. Let's start with the important ones:

`package.json`

This file is our project's heart, storing all the dependencies and scripts needed for our application to run. You'll notice that we're using Vue version 3, listed as a dependency. We also have some Vue CLI and ESLint dev dependencies.

The scripts section is really handy:

- `serve`: Runs our application.
- `build`: Builds our application for production.
- `lint`: Fixes any linting errors in our code.

We also have a configuration file for ESLint, which helps keep our code tidy and consistent. You can see how straightforward it is to manage our dependencies and scripts with `package.json`.

yarn.lock

Based on your preference for package managers, you might see either a yarn.lock or package-lock.json file. These files ensure that we always install the exact same versions of our dependencies, no matter who is working on the project. Think of it as a way to keep things consistent and avoid surprises!

babel.config.js

This file handles our Babel configuration. Babel is a tool that converts our modern JavaScript code, which some older browsers might not understand, into an older version that works everywhere. This babel.config.js file uses the Vue CLI Babel preset, which makes sure everything is set up for us.

node_modules

This folder contains all the dependencies that our project needs. When you run vue create or npm install, these packages get downloaded and placed in this folder. It's like a library of tools that our application uses!

public

This folder holds the static assets that will be served when our application goes live. It includes two files:
- favicon.ico: This is the little icon you see in your browser tab. It's not specific to Vue.
- index.html: This is the **only** HTML file in our Vue application. We're building single-page applications, so this is the core of our structure.

While we might add some changes to the head tag of index.html, we don't touch the body. We want Vue to control our user interface, and that's where our next folder comes in…

src

This is the folder where most of our development time will be spent. This is the heart of our Vue application.

`main.js`

This is the starting point for our application. Here, we tell Vue which component is our root component (the `App` component), and which DOM element Vue should control. Remember, that DOM element is our `div` with in `index.html`. We call this element the root DOM node because Vue will manage everything inside it.

`App.vue`

This file represents our root component. It's where we define the HTML, CSS, and JavaScript that make up the core of our user interface. The `App` component is rendered inside the root DOM node we talked about earlier.

`components`

This folder is where we store our reusable components. Components are like building blocks that we can reuse throughout our application. In our Hello World example, we have a component called `HelloWorld.vue` that handles the welcome message.

`assets`

This folder is for storing images, SVGs, or other assets that we need in our application. It's a convenient place to keep things organized.

Single File Components

Before we dive into the heart of Vue.js, there's one more essential piece of the puzzle we need to understand: the **.vue file**. In in the previous section, I briefly mentioned it, but now let's take a closer look.

A .vue file is a special file type that uses HTML-like syntax to define a part of your user interface. Think of it as a building block for your Vue app. For instance, in our "Hello World" project, we have two .vue files: `app.vue`, responsible for the logo, and `helloworld.vue`, responsible for the links. So each .vue file is responsible for a specific portion of your app's interface.

Now let's open up a .vue file and see what's inside! Every .vue file is made up of three main sections:

- **The** `template` **Block:** This is like the HTML of your UI. It defines the structure and layout of your component.
- **The** `script` **Block:** This is where you define the data and logic for your component. Think of it as the JavaScript part of your UI.
- **The** `style` **Block:** This is where you add CSS styles that affect the HTML elements defined in your `template` block.

Here's a simple example:

```
<template>
  <h1>Hello World</h1>
</template>

<script>
export default {
  data() {
    return {
      message: 'This is a message from the script block!'
    }
  }
}
</script>

<style>
h1 {
  color: blue;
}
</style>
```

This code defines a simple component with a heading that says "Hello World". It also includes a variable `message` in the `script` block and styles the heading with blue text. The browser doesn't understand .vue files directly, so **webpack** with the **vue-loader** takes care of processing this file. It extracts each block, applies necessary transformations, and finally compiles everything into a format the browser understands.

Now, let's talk about **components**. You might have noticed a folder named `components` in our project. This is where we store our .vue files, which are also known as Single File Components (SFCs).

When we talk about "components" in Vue, we're usually referring to .vue files. However, as beginners, we don't need to worry about the intricate details of component architecture right away. We'll focus on learning the fundamentals by working with a single .vue file. Later in the series, we'll dive deep into the world of components and their power.

For now, let's delete the `components` folder with all its contents, and the related code in the `script` block from `app.vue`. We'll also remove the logo to have a clean slate. Don't worry, we'll come back to components later!

We will now have:

```
<template>

</template>

<script>
export default {
  name: 'App',

}
</script>

<style>
#app {
  font-family: Avenir, Helvetica, Arial, sans-serif;
  -webkit-font-smoothing: antialiased;
  -moz-osx-font-smoothing: grayscale;
  text-align: center;
  color: #2c3e50;
  margin-top: 60px;
}
</style>
```

Earlier, we talked about how the `script` block handles data and logic for the `template` block, but how does this connection work?

The `script` block exports a default object that can have a property called `data`. This `data` property is a function that returns an object containing data that the `template` block can access. For instance, if we want to display a name in our HTML, we would add a key-value pair like `name: "Developer"` to the `data` object.

The key part is understanding how to connect this data in the `script` block to the HTML elements in the `template` block. This is called **declarative programming**. We tell Vue how we want to bind our data to the HTML, and Vue takes care of the rest.

Binding in Vue

Binding Text

W have explored single-file components. Remember, these are like the building blocks of our Vue.js apps, each one handling its own piece of the user interface. We also learned that a component has three main parts: the template (which controls how things look), the script (where we store the data and logic), and the style (for styling).

Now, we're going to dive into how to connect the data in our script to the template. Think of it like having a backstage area (the script) where we store all the information, and a stage (the template) where we present it to the audience. We need a way to bring that information from backstage to the stage, and that's where text binding comes in.

Imagine we have a simple greeting in our template:

```
<div>Hello Developer</div>
```

If we save this and open our browser, we see "Hello Developer" displayed. But what if we want this greeting to be dynamic? What if we want to display different names based on user input or data from an API?

That's where the mustache syntax comes in. This is Vue's way of connecting data to our template. It looks like this: {{ }}. Inside these curly braces, we write the name of the data property we want to display.

Let's say we have a `name` property in our script:

```
<script>
export default {
  name: 'App',
  data() {
  return {
    name: 'Developer'
  }
}
}
</script>
```

Now, in our template, we can replace "Developer" with the mustache syntax:

```
<template>
```

```
<div>Hello {{ name }}</div>

</template>
```

Save and refresh the browser! You'll see "Hello Developer" still. But now, if you change the value of name in your script to "Batman," you'll see the greeting change to "Hello Batman" on the browser without refreshing the page! This dynamic update is the beauty of text binding!

This process is called **text interpolation.** Vue.js effectively replaces the mustache syntax with the actual value of the data property at runtime. It's like a magic trick where the content changes automatically based on our backstage data.

You can use the mustache syntax within larger strings too. For example:

```
<template>
<div>My name is {{ name }} and I like to code!</div>
</template>
```

Or, the mustache syntax can be the only content of an HTML element:

```
<div>{{ name }}</div>
```

You can also use multiple mustache expressions in a single element:

```
<template>
<div>{{ greet }} {{ name }}</div>
</template>

<script>
export default {
  name: 'App',
data() {
  return {
    name: 'Batman',
    greet: 'Hello'
  }
}
}
</script>
```

This will display "Hello Batman" in the browser.

The v-text Directive: Another Way to Bind Text

Besides the mustache syntax, Vue.js provides a special HTML attribute called a directive. Directives are like special instructions that tell Vue.js how to handle certain elements. They have the prefix `v-`. For text binding, we use the `v-text` directive.

Let's say we have another data property called `book`:

```
data() {
  return {
    book: "Developer's Guide"
  }
}
```

We can use the `v-text` directive to bind this to an element:

```
<div v-text="book"></div>
```

The `v-text` directive will replace the entire inner text of the element with the value of the `book` property. So, we'll see "Developer's Guide" displayed in the browser.

Choosing the Right Tool for the Job

The main drawback of the `v-text` directive is that it replaces the entire content of the element. So, if you want to mix static text and dynamic data, the mustache syntax is the way to go.

Let's say you want to display "Hello Batman" but only use the `v-text` directive with the `name` property. This won't work:

```
<div>Hello <div v-text="name"></div></div>
```

You'll get an error: "v-text will overwrite element children".

So, to summarize:

- **Mustache syntax (`{{ }}`)**: For partial or full text binding, allowing for mixed static and dynamic content.
- **v-text directive**: For replacing the entire text content of an element with a single data property.

The mustache syntax is generally preferred for its flexibility and speed. While `v-text` has its place, it's not as common in day-to-day Vue.js development.

Exercise:

Create a new component with two data properties: `firstName` and `lastName`. Use both the mustache syntax and the `v-text` directive to display a full name in different elements.

Solution:

```
<template>
  <div>
    <div>My full name is: {{ firstName }}
{{ lastName }}</div>
    <div v-text="firstName + ' ' + lastName"></div>
  </div>
</template>

<script>
export default {
  data() {
    return {
      firstName: 'Bruce',
      lastName: 'Wayne'
    }
  }
}
</script>
```

This example demonstrates the flexibility of both methods. The mustache syntax allows for dynamic parts within a larger static string, while `v-text` replaces the entire content of the element with the combined value.

Remember, practice makes perfect! Experiment with these different text binding techniques and see what works best for your projects. We'll explore more advanced data binding concepts in our upcoming chapters.

Binding HTML

In our last chapter, we learned about the trusty mustache syntax and the `v-text` directive, which are great for binding data to the UI. But what happens when we need to render real HTML in the UI? Let's say you're building a form where users can enter text using a rich text editor, with options to bold, italicize, and more. Imagine wanting to display this input in a read-only mode, maintaining all the formatting the user added. That's where the `v-html` directive comes in handy!

Let's dive into an example. We'll create a data property that holds a string enclosed within bold tags. Let's give our `book` property the value "Developer's Guide", wrapped with a bold tag. If we try to bind this data using either the mustache syntax or the `v-text` directive, we'll notice that the value gets rendered as plain text. The bold tag will appear as text on the UI, not actually making the text bold.

To render the HTML properly, we need to swap to the `v-html` directive. Let's get rid of the mustache syntax, which isn't going to work here, and change `v-text` to `v-html`.

```
<template>
  <div>
    <div v-html="message"></div>
  </div>
</template>

<script>
export default {
  data() {
    return {
      message: "<b>Developer's Guide</b>"
    };
}};
</script>
```

 Save the file, head over to the browser, and – Voilà! You'll see the book name rendered in bold.

Remember, the `v-html` directive is your go-to when you need to render real HTML in your application. But there's a crucial warning: always be mindful of the content you're rendering.

Think of it like this: If you're using a third-party API, rendering content from it using `v-html` can be risky. It could open the door for nasty cross-site scripting (XSS) attacks. XSS attacks let bad actors inject malicious code into your application, potentially putting your users' information at risk.

Let's visualize this. Imagine we have a data property called `hack` that holds an anchor tag. This tag, when clicked, triggers a change: "Enter your password!" The anchor text itself will say "Win a prize."

```
<template>
  <div>
    <div @click="message = `Enter a Passord:<input
type=number>`" v-          html="message">
    </div>
  </div>
</template>
```

```
<script>
export default {
  data() {
    return {
      message: "<a href='/'>Welcome to My Website</a>"
    };
  },
};
</script>
```

If we bind this data to our template using `v-html`, save the file, and head to the browser, we'll see the link "Win a prize." Clicking it, unfortunately, will display the dreaded "Enter your Password" message.

While this is simple, it highlights the potential danger. Imagine if a hacker could inject something much more harmful than a simple alert. It's crucial to treat user-provided data with caution and sanitize it before using `v-html`.

So, while the `v-html` directive is a powerful tool for rendering HTML, always remember to exercise caution and sanitize the content you're rendering. This will keep your users safe and prevent potentially harmful scripts from infiltrating your application.

Exercise:

Create a new Vue component with a data property named `message` holding the following HTML string:

```
<h1>Welcome to My Website</h1>
<p>This is a simple example of rendering HTML using v-
html.</p>
```

Use the `v-html` directive to display this HTML in the template of your component.

Solution:

```
<template>
  <div>
    <div v-html="message"></div>
  </div>
</template>

<script>
export default {
  data() {
    return {
```

```
      message: '<h1>Welcome to My Website</h1><p>This is a
simple example of rendering HTML using v-html.</p>'
    };
  },
};
</script>
```

You'll see the heading and paragraph rendered as actual HTML elements in your browser.

Binding to Attributes

Let's dive into a super helpful feature in Vue.js called "attribute binding." It's a way to connect our dynamic data to HTML attributes. Think of it like a bridge between our Vue.js world and the HTML world, making things interactive!

Imagine you want to change an element's `id`, `class`, or even make a button disabled or enabled. Attribute binding is our secret weapon for this.

First, let's add a new data property to our Vue component. This property will store the `id` we want to give to an element:

```
data() {
  return {
    headingId: 'myHeading' // Our dynamic ID
  };
}
```

Now, in our template, we'll use the `v-bind` directive to connect this data property (`headingId`) to the `id` attribute of an `<h2>` tag:

```
<template>
  <h2>{{ headingId }}</h2>
  <h2 v-bind:id="headingId">Heading</h2>
</template>
```

Explanation:

- `v-bind:id="headingId"`: This line is our key. It says: "Bind the value of the `headingId` property to the `id` attribute of this `<h2>` tag."
- `<h2>{{ headingId }}</h2>`: This just displays the text "Heading" as the heading.

Save your file and see the magic! You should see an `<h2>` element with the `id` set to `myHeading`. If you inspect it in your browser's developer tools, you'll confirm that the `id` is correctly assigned.

Binding to Boolean Attributes

Imagine we want a button that can be disabled or enabled based on some condition. Enter the `v-bind` directive again!

Add a new data property for our button's disabled state:

```
data() {
  return {
    headingId: 'myHeading',
    isDisabled: true // Our button is initially disabled
  };
}
```

Then, in our template, let's create a button and use `v-bind` to connect the `isDisabled` property to the `disabled` attribute:

```
<template>
  <button v-bind:disabled="isDisabled">Click Me</button>
</template>
```

Now, if you refresh your browser, the button will be disabled. Cool, right?

Here's the cool part. If you change the value of `isDisabled` to `false` in your Vue component's script, the button will instantly become enabled! This is the power of dynamic binding in action.

When using `v-bind` with boolean attributes (like `disabled`), there's a special rule. If the bound property is `false`, the attribute will be removed from the HTML element. This is because the very existence of the attribute is what makes it "true" in HTML.

Let's say you have a checkbox:

```
<input type="checkbox" v-bind:disabled="isDisabled">
```

If `isDisabled` is `false`, the checkbox will be enabled, and you won't see the `disabled` attribute in the HTML. But if `isDisabled` is `true`, you'll see `disabled` attribute in the HTML.

Attribute binding isn't just for `id` and `disabled`. It's also your best friend for changing the look and feel of your elements using the `class` and `style` attributes.

Exercise 1: Create a new component with a paragraph (`<p>`). Add a data property called `textColor` and set it to `"blue"`. Use `v-bind` to bind the `textColor` property to the `style` attribute of the paragraph and set the `color` property to the `textColor`.

Exercise 2: Create a new component with a button. Add a data property called isRed and set it to false. Use v-bind to bind the isRed property to the class attribute of the button. Add a CSS class called .red with the style background-color: red. Make the button turn red when isRed is true.

Binding Classes

Imagine you're building a website where you need to dynamically change the look of elements based on user interaction or data changes. This is where class binding comes in handy!

In Vue.js, we use the v-bind directive to bind attributes to our elements, and we can use this to manipulate an element's classes. Let's start with a basic example:

```
<template>
  <div >
    <h2 class="underline">Underlined Text</h2>
  </div>
</template>

<style>
.underline {
  text-decoration: underline;
}
</style>
```

This code creates an h2 element with the class underline. We've defined the underline class in our CSS, which adds an underline to the text.

Now, what if we want to change this class dynamically? We can use the v-bind directive and a data property. Let's add a data property called status that can hold different values like danger or success:

```
<template>
  <div >
    <h2 v-bind:class="status">Status: {{ status }}</h2>
  </div>
</template>

<script>
export default {
  data() {
    return {
      status: "danger",
```

```
      };
    },
  };
</script>

<style>
.danger {
  color: red;
}

.success {
  color: green;
}
</style>
```

Now, when the `status` is `danger`, the h2 element will have the class `danger` and the text will turn red. If we change `status` to `success`, the text will turn green!

Conditional Class Binding

What if we want to apply classes based on specific conditions? We can achieve this using conditional statements or the ternary operator.

Let's say we want to apply the `promoted` class if a movie is promoted:

```
<template>
  <div >
    <h2 v-bind:class="{ promoted: isPromoted }">Promoted
Movie</h2>
  </div>
</template>

<script>
export default {
  data() {
    return {
      isPromoted: true,
    };
  },
};
</script>

<style>
.promoted {
  font-style: italic;
}
</style>
```

The :class directive is used to bind the promoted class to the h2 element. If the isPromoted data property is true, the promoted class will be applied, and the text will be italicized.

We can also use the ternary operator to conditionally apply multiple classes:

```
<template>
  <div >
    <h2 v-bind:class="[isSoldOut ? 'sold-out' :
'new']">Possible Sold Out Movie</h2>
  </div>
</template>

<script>
export default {
  data() {
    return {
      isSoldOut: true,
    };
  },
};
</script>

<style>
.sold-out {
  color: red;
}

.new {
  color: green;
}
</style>
```

In this example, if isSoldOut is true, the sold-out class will be applied, making the text red. Otherwise, the new class will be applied, turning the text green.

Binding Classes with Arrays and Objects

We can also apply classes by binding arrays and objects to the :class directive. Using an array, we can apply multiple classes at once:

```
<template>
  <div >
    <h2 v-bind:class="['new', 'promoted']">Newly Promoted
Movie</h2>
  </div>
```

```
</template>
```

In this example, both the new and promoted classes will be applied to the h2 element.

With objects, we can specify conditions for applying each class:

```
<template>
  <div >
    <h2 v-bind:class="{ promoted: isPromoted, new: !
isSoldOut, 'sold-out': isSoldOut }">Object Conditional
Movie</h2>
  </div>
</template>
```

In this example, the promoted class will be applied if isPromoted is true, the new class will be applied if isSoldOut is false, and the sold-out class will be applied if isSoldOut is true.

Exercise

Create a simple Vue.js component that displays a message with different styles based on a data property called messageType. The messageType property can have three values: info, warning, or error.

Apply the following CSS classes conditionally:

- **info**: blue text, background color light blue.
- **warning**: yellow text, background color light yellow.
- **error**: red text, background color light red.

Solution:

```
<template>
  <div >
    <div v-bind:class="{ info: messageType === 'info',
warning: messageType === 'warning', error: messageType ===
'error' }">
      {{ message }}
    </div>
  </div>
</template>

<script>
export default {
  data() {
    return {
      message: "This is an info message",
      messageType: "info",
```

```
      };
    },
  };
</script>

<style>
.info {
  color: blue;
  background-color: lightblue;
}

.warning {
  color: yellow;
  background-color: lightyellow;
}

.error {
  color: red;
  background-color: lightred;
}
</style>
```

And that's it! You've learned the basics of binding classes in Vue.js 3, allowing you to dynamically style your components and create dynamic user interfaces. Practice these concepts and experiment with different ways to use class binding to improve your Vue.js projects.

Binding Styles

Even though it's generally better to use CSS classes for styling, we sometimes need to use inline styles. In this section, we'll learn how to bind inline styles in Vue.js.

There are two ways to bind styles: using the object syntax and the array syntax. Let's start with the object syntax.

Object Syntax

The object syntax, as the name suggests, binds the `style` attribute to a JavaScript object. Let's say we have an `h2` tag with the text "Inline Style" and want to bind a color to it.

First, we declare a data property called `highlightColor` and set its value to "orange."

```
data() {
```

```
  return {
    highlightColor: "orange",
  };
},
```

Now, to bind this color, we use the `v-bind` directive. We bind the `style` attribute to a JavaScript object. This object will have key-value pairs, where the key is the CSS property and the value is the data property we declared.

```
<h2 v-bind:style="{ color: highlightColor }">Inline
Style</h2>
```

If you save this code and view it in the browser, you'll see the heading is orange. Inspecting the element in the browser will reveal that the `color: orange` style has been applied as an inline style.

Let's add another property, `headerSize`, to our data object and set it to 50. We can then add this to our style object.

```
data() {
  return {
    highlightColor: "orange",
    headerSize: 50,
  };
},
<h2 v-bind:style="{ color: highlightColor, 'font-size':
headerSize + 'px' }">Inline Style</h2>
```

Notice that we wrapped the `font-size` property in quotes, since it's a hyphenated style. We also appended "px" to the `headerSize` value to ensure it's treated as a pixel value. If you refresh the browser, you'll see the new font size of 50 pixels applied.

For hyphenated styles, also known as kebab-cased styles, Vue.js also allows you to specify the style in camel case. You could use `fontSize` instead of `'font-size'`, and the browser output would remain unchanged.

You can also include static values in your style object. For example, you could set the padding to `20px` directly:

```
<h2 v-bind:style="{ color: highlightColor, 'font-size':
headerSize + 'px', padding: '20px' }">Inline Style</h2>
```

This approach works well for simple inline styles, but as the number of properties increases, the template can become cluttered.

Style Object Approach

For cleaner templates, Vue.js allows us to bind a style object directly.

Let's create a data property called `headerStyle` and assign it an object containing CSS properties as key-value pairs.

```
data() {
  return {
    headerStyle: {
      color: "orange",
      'font-size': '50px',
      padding: '20px',
    },
  };
},
```

Now we can create an `h2` tag that uses this style object:

```
<h2 v-bind:style="headerStyle">Style Object</h2>
```

This `h2` tag will display the same styles as the previous example, but the template is much cleaner. If you have multiple inline styles, the style object approach is definitely recommended.

Array Syntax

The array syntax for the `style` attribute allows you to apply multiple style objects to the same element. Let's create two style objects: `baseStyle` and `successStyle`.

```
data() {
  return {
    baseStyle: {
      'font-size': '16px',
      padding: '10px',
    },
    successStyle: {
      color: 'green',
      'background-color': 'lightgreen',
      border: '2px solid green',
    },
  };
},
```

We can then bind both of these style objects to a `div` tag using an array:

```
<div v-bind:style="[baseStyle, successStyle]">Success
Style</div>
```

This will apply both `baseStyle` and `successStyle` to the `div`.

An important point to remember is that styles in the last style object override any conflicting styles in the previous style objects. For example, if we add a padding of `20px` to the `successStyle` object, the `div` will have a padding of `20px` even though the `baseStyle` object had a different padding.

```
data() {
  return {
    baseStyle: {
      'font-size': '16px',
      padding: '10px',
    },
    successStyle: {
      color: 'green',
      'background-color': 'lightgreen',
      border: '2px solid green',
      padding: '20px',
    },
  };
},
```

You can use this array syntax to apply multiple styles and control the order of precedence.

Exercise

Try creating a `div` element that displays the following styles:

- **Base style:** font-size: 14px, padding: 5px, border: 1px solid gray
- **Warning style:** background-color: yellow, color: black, border: 2px solid orange

Solution:

```
data() {
  return {
    baseStyle: {
      'font-size': '14px',
      padding: '5px',
      border: '1px solid gray',
    },
    warningStyle: {
      'background-color': 'yellow',
      color: 'black',
      border: '2px solid orange',
```

```
      },
    };
  },
<div v-bind:style="[baseStyle, warningStyle]">Warning
Message</div>
```

That's it for binding inline styles in Vue.js! Remember, while it's generally best to use CSS classes, sometimes you'll need to use inline styles. Vue.js makes it easy to bind these styles to your components using either the object syntax or the array syntax.

v-bind Shorthand

We've been working with the v-bind directive a lot, and it's a real workhorse for making our components dynamic. But typing out v-bind all the time can feel a bit repetitive, right?

Well, Vue has a super handy shorthand that saves us some keystrokes. Instead of writing v-bind:attributeName, we can simply use a colon followed by the attribute name: :attributeName. That's it! Vue knows exactly what we're trying to do.

Think about it this way - the colon is like a shortcut code that says, "Hey Vue, bind this attribute to this expression."

Let's see it in actione. v-bind to dynamically change the src attribute of an image?

```
<template>
  <img :src="imageUrl" alt="Dynamic Image">
</template>

<script>
export default {
  data() {
    return {
      imageUrl: 'https://www.example.com/image.jpg'
    }
  }
}
</script>
```

Here, :src is the shorthand for v-bind:src. This code still achieves the same result.

The best part? This shorthand is the standard way to use v-bind in Vue projects. Most developers use it, so getting comfortable with it is super important.

Now, you might be wondering why we didn't start with the shorthand. The reason is simple - I wanted you to understand the concept of `v-bind` first. It's important to know what's happening behind the scenes before using a shortcut!

Think of it like learning to ride a bicycle. You start with training wheels and then learn to balance on your own. The `v-bind` directive is like those training wheels, helping you understand the concept of attribute binding before we dive into the more common shorthand.

Rendering

Conditional Rendering

In this section, we're going to dive into a really useful feature in Vue.js – conditional rendering. Imagine you're building a website, and you want to show different parts of it depending on whether a user is logged in or not, or maybe you want to display a special offer only to certain users. This is where conditional rendering comes in.

Vue.js makes conditional rendering super easy. We're going to learn about three main directives: v-if, v-else, and v-else-if. These directives let us control which parts of our HTML are shown based on different conditions.

Let's start with a simple example. Let's say we have a variable called num and we want to display different messages based on its value:

- If num is 0, we want to show "The number is zero."
- If num is positive, we want to show "The number is positive."
- If num is negative, we want to show "The number is negative."
- If num is not a number, we want to show "Not a number."

Here's how we can achieve this:

```
<template>
  <div>
    <h2 v-if="num === 0">The number is zero</h2>
    <h2 v-else-if="num > 0">The number is positive</h2>
    <h2 v-else-if="num < 0">The number is negative</h2>
    <h2 v-else>Not a number</h2>
  </div>
</template>

<script>
export default {
  data() {
    return {
      num: 0
    };
  }
};
</script>
```

In our template, we have four h2 tags. Each tag uses one of the directives we learned:

- `v-if="num === 0"`: This displays the "The number is zero" message **only** if the value of `num` is exactly 0.
- `v-else-if="num > 0"`: This displays the "The number is positive" message if `num` is greater than 0, but **only** if the previous `v-if` condition was false.
- `v-else-if="num < 0"`: This displays the "The number is negative" message if `num` is less than 0, but **only** if the previous `v-if` and `v-else-if` conditions were false.
- `v-else`: This displays the "Not a number" message if **none** of the previous conditions are true.

When you run this code, you'll see the message corresponding to the current value of `num`. If you change `num` in your JavaScript code, the displayed message will automatically update!

Exercise:

Try modifying the code to display different messages based on the following conditions:

- If `num` is even, display "The number is even".
- If `num` is odd, display "The number is odd".
- If `num` is a multiple of 5, display "The number is a multiple of 5".

Solution:

```
<template>
  <div>
    <h2 v-if="num % 2 === 0">The number is even</h2>
    <h2 v-else-if="num % 2 !== 0">The number is odd</h2>
    <h2 v-else-if="num % 5 === 0">The number is a multiple
of 5</h2>
    <h2 v-else>Not a number</h2>
  </div>
</template>

<script>
export default {
  data() {
    return {
      num: 0
    };
  }
};
</script>
```

In this solution, we use the modulo operator (%) to check if the number is even (remainder is 0 when divided by 2), odd (remainder is not 0 when divided by 2), or a multiple of 5 (remainder is 0 when divided by 5).

Imagine you have a heading (an h2 element) that you want to show or hide based on some condition. We can achieve this with v-show. Let's create a simple example:

```
<template>
  <div>
    <h2 v-show="showElement">
      Using v-show
    </h2>
  </div>
</template>

<script>
export default {
  data() {
    return {
      showElement: true,
    };
  },
};
</script>
```

Now, if we open our browser, we'll see the h2 element because showElement is true. If we change showElement to false in our code, the heading will disappear.

You might be wondering, "Wait, doesn't v-if do the same thing?" You're right, both v-if and v-show can hide and show elements. But there's a key difference.

Let's illustrate this by duplicating our h2 element and using v-if instead of v-show. We'll keep showElement set to true so both elements are initially visible:

```
<template>
  <div>
    <h2 v-show="showElement">
      Using v-show
    </h2>
    <h2 v-if="showElement">
      Using v-if
    </h2>
  </div>
</template>
```

```
<script>
export default {
  data() {
    return {
      showElement: true,
    };
  },
};
</script>
```

Now, let's look at the browser's "Inspect Element" tool. You'll see both `h2` elements in the DOM, one with `v-show` and the other with `v-if`. If we change `showElement` to `false`, the `h2` element with `v-if` will completely disappear from the DOM, while the one with `v-show` will remain in the DOM, but with its `display` style set to `none`.

So, when should you use `v-if` versus `v-show`?

- `v-if`: Use it when the condition is unlikely to change frequently, or when you have multiple elements that depend on the same condition. It's more efficient to remove and add elements from the DOM when the condition changes.
- `v-show`: Use it when the condition changes frequently or you want to quickly toggle the visibility of an element. This is more efficient for simply hiding or showing an element without removing it from the DOM.

Now that you're familiar with `v-show`, you have four directives at your disposal for conditional rendering in Vue: `v-if`, `v-else-if`, `v-else`, and `v-show`. Remember, conditional rendering is essential for creating dynamic and user-friendly web applications, so make sure you understand how each of these directives works.

List Rendering

Imagine you're building an online store. You need to show all the products, right? That's a list! Or maybe you're creating a social media app. You'll need to show a list of posts.

Vue.js makes handling lists easy using the `v-for` directive. It's like a magic wand for repeating HTML elements. We'll be exploring different scenarios with `v-for` to see how it works with arrays, objects, and even nested lists.

Simple String Arrays

Let's start with a simple list of names.:

```
data() {
  return {
    names: ['Bruce', 'Clark', 'Diana'],
  };
},
```

Now, we want to display these names in our HTML. This is where the `v-for` directive comes in:

```
<template>
  <div>
    <h2>Names:</h2>
    <h2 v-for="name in names" :key="name">{{ name }}</h2>
  </div>
</template>
```

Let's break down this code:

- `<h2 v-for="name in names" :key="name">{{ name }}</h2>`: This line is the heart of our list rendering. The `v-for` directive tells Vue to repeat the `<h2>` tag for each item in the `names` array.
  - `name in names`: We assign the current item in the array to a variable called `name`.
  - `:key="name"`: This is the `key` attribute. It's super important! Think of it as a unique identifier for each item in the list. Vue uses this to track changes and efficiently update the list when needed.
  - `{{ name }}`: This is the mustache syntax, which displays the value of the `name` variable.

Save your file and take a look at your browser. You should see the names "Bruce," "Clark," and "Diana" displayed in a list. Awesome!

Accessing Index

Sometimes, you might want to know the index (position) of each item in your list. You can access this information within the `v-for` loop using `index`. Let's modify our example to show the index:

```
<template>
  <div>
    <h2>Names:</h2>
    <h2 v-for="(name, index) in
names" :key="name">{{ index }} - {{ name }}</h2>
```

```
    </div>
</template>
```

Now, our output will look like this:

```
0 - Bruce
1 - Clark
2 - Diana
```

Iterating Over Objects

Now, let's get fancier and work with an array of objects. Update your `data` property:

```
data() {
  return {
    fullNames: [
      { firstName: 'Bruce', lastName: 'Wayne' },
      { firstName: 'Clark', lastName: 'Kent' },
      { firstName: 'Princess', lastName: 'Diana' },
    ],
  };
},
```

In our template, we'll use the `v-for` directive to loop over each object in the `fullNames` array and display the first and last name:

```
<template>
  <div>
    <h2>Full Names:</h2>
    <h2 v-for="(name, index) in
fullNames" :key="name.firstName">
        {{ index }} - {{ name.firstName }} {{ name.lastName }}
    </h2>
  </div>
</template>
```

Notice that we are using the object's `firstName` property as the `key` since it's unique for each object.

Nested Lists

Let's ramp up the complexity a bit more. We'll create a list of actors and their movies. Add this new data property to your component:

```
data() {
  return {
    actors: [
      { name: 'Christian Bale', movies: ['Batman', 'The
Prestige'] },
```

```
    { name: 'Leonardo DiCaprio', movies: ['Titanic',
'Inception'] },
    ],
  };
},
```

To display this data, we'll use nested `v-for` loops:

```
<template>
  <div>
    <h2>Actors:</h2>
    <div v-for="actor in actors" :key="actor.name">
      <h3>{{ actor.name }}</h3>
      <ul>
        <li v-for="(movie, movieIndex) in
actor.movies" :key="movie">
          {{ movieIndex }} - {{ movie }}
        </li>
      </ul>
    </div>
  </div>
</template>
```

This code iterates over each actor and then loops through the `movies` array within that actor's object.

Iterating Over Object Properties

The `v-for` directive isn't just for arrays. You can also use it to iterate over the properties of an object. Let's add another `data` property to demonstrate:

```
data() {
  return {
    myInfo: {
      name: 'Developer',
      book: "Developer's Guide",
      course: 'Vue 3',
    },
  };
},
```

In the template, we'll use `v-for` to display each key-value pair:

```
<template>
  <div>
    <h2>My Info:</h2>
    <h2 v-for="(value, key, index) in myInfo" :key="key">
      {{ index }} - {{ key }}: {{ value }}
    </h2>
```

```
    </div>
  </template>
```

Here, we are accessing the `value`, `key`, and `index` of each property in the `myInfo` object.

Template Tag

Sometimes, you'll want to render multiple HTML elements within the `v-for` loop. You can achieve this using the `<template>` tag:

```
<template>
  <div>
    <h2>Names:</h2>
    <template v-for="name in names" :key="name">
      <h2>{{ name }}</h2>
      <hr>
    </template>
  </div>
</template>
```

This will render each name followed by a horizontal line (`<hr>`). Remember, the `<template>` tag itself won't be rendered in the DOM.

Key Attribute: A Closer Look

You've seen the `key` attribute being used throughout this chapter. It's not just a formality; it plays a crucial role in Vue's list rendering performance. When you modify a list, Vue uses the `key` attribute to figure out which items have changed, been added, or removed. This allows it to update the list efficiently without having to re-render the entire thing. It's like a secret code that tells Vue how to manage your list, so make sure you provide a unique `key` for each item!

Conditional List Rendering

We can use the `v-for` directive to loop through an array and show each item. But what if we only want to show certain items from that list? That's where **conditional list rendering** comes in!

Let's say we have an array of names:

```
data() {
  return {
    names: ['Bruce', 'Clark', 'Diana'],
```

```
  };
},
```

We want to display only the name "Bruce" in our UI. We can do this with a little help from the `v-if` directive. Here's how we would normally do it:

```
<template>
  <div>
    <ul>
      <li v-for="(name, index) in names" :key="index">
        <h2 v-if="name === 'Bruce'">{{ name }}</h2>
      </li>
    </ul>
  </div>
</template>
```

This would display a list of all the names, but only the "Bruce" name would be shown inside an `<h2>` tag, since the `v-if` directive checks if the name is equal to "Bruce."

However, our trusty friend **eslint** might raise a flag here! It will tell us that we can't mix `v-for` and `v-if` directives like this. The reason is that Vue evaluates `v-if` before `v-for`, so the name variable doesn't exist yet when `v-if` tries to check it. This creates a bit of a problem.

So, how do we fix this? Well, there are a couple of ways. One solution is using **computed properties**, which we will learn about later. For now, let's focus on another solution: **template tags!**

Instead of putting the `v-if` on the h2 element, we'll wrap it in a template tag:

```
<template>
  <div>
    <ul>
      <li v-for="(name, index) in names" :key="index">
        <template v-if="name === 'Bruce'">
          <h2>{{ name }}</h2>
        </template>
      </li>
    </ul>
  </div>
</template>
```

This way, the `v-if` directive checks the condition *inside* the template tag, after `v-for` has created the name variable. This keeps eslint happy and our code working as expected!

Now if you run this code, you'll only see the name "Bruce" displayed in the `<h2>` tag.

Remember, this is just one example of conditional list rendering. You can use this technique with any kind of data and any condition you need to check.

Exercise:

You have an array of fruits:

```
data() {
  return {
    names: ['apple', 'banana', 'orange', 'grape'],
  };
},
```

Use conditional list rendering to show only the fruits that start with the letter 'b'.

Solution:

```
<template>
  <div>
    <ul>
      <li v-for="(fruit, index) in fruits" :key="index">
        <template v-if="fruit.startsWith('b')">
          <h2>{{ fruit }}</h2>
        </template>
      </li>
    </ul>
  </div>
</template>
```

So, with a little creativity and the help of `v-if` and template tags, we can create dynamic lists that adapt to our needs. Now, let's move on to learning about methods in Vue!

Exercise

Create a simple shopping cart app. You'll have a list of items, each with a name, price, and quantity. Use the `v-for` directive to display these items in a table. Calculate the total price of the cart and display it below the table.

Solution:

```
data() {
  return {
```

```
    cartItems: [
      { name: 'Laptop', price: 1200, quantity: 1 },
      { name: 'Keyboard', price: 80, quantity: 2 },
      { name: 'Mouse', price: 30, quantity: 1 },
    ],
  };
},
<template>
  <div>
    <h2>Shopping Cart</h2>
    <table>
      <thead>
        <tr>
          <th>Name</th>
          <th>Price</th>
          <th>Quantity</th>
          <th>Subtotal</th>
        </tr>
      </thead>
      <tbody>
        <tr v-for="(item, index) in cartItems" :key="index">
          <td>{{ item.name }}</td>
          <td>{{ item.price }}</td>
          <td>{{ item.quantity }}</td>
          <td>{{ item.price * item.quantity }}</td>
        </tr>
      </tbody>
    </table>
    <p>Total Price: {{ calculateTotalPrice() }}</p>
  </div>
</template>
methods: {
  calculateTotalPrice() {
    let total = 0;
    for (const item of this.cartItems) {
      total += item.price * item.quantity;
    }
    return total;
  },
},
```

Methods

Imagine you're building a simple app that needs to add up numbers. You can do this directly in your template, but what if you need to reuse this calculation? That's where methods shine!

Let's start with an empty `App.vue` file. We'll create a simple example to get started.

```
<template>
  <div>
    <h2>{{ 2 + 3 + 5 }}</h2>
  </div>
</template>

<script>
export default {
  // We'll add our methods here later
};
</script>
```

If we open this in our browser, we'll see the result, `10`. Now, let's say we need to add a different set of numbers: `5 + 10 + 15`. We could copy and paste the expression, but that's not very efficient. It's like writing the same instructions over and over!

This is where methods come in. They're like little helpers that encapsulate reusable logic. Let's create a method called `add` in our `App.vue` file:

```
<template>
  <div>
    <h2>{{ add(2, 3, 5) }}</h2>
  </div>
</template>

<script>
export default {
  methods: {
    add(a, b, c) {
      return a + b + c;
    }
  }
};
</script>
```

Now we can call `add(2, 3, 5)` in our template, and it will return the result, `10`. This way, we can use the same method to add different numbers without repeating ourselves.

You'll notice we define methods within a `methods` object in the `script` section. These functions are called "methods" because they're associated with the component object.

Now let's make our `add` method a bit more dynamic by adding parameters:

```
<template>
  <div>
    <h2>{{ add(2, 3, 5) }}</h2>
    <h2>{{ add(10, 15, 20) }}</h2>
  </div>
</template>

<script>
export default {
  methods: {
    add(a, b, c) {
      return a + b + c;
    }
  }
};
</script>
```

Now, we've created a truly reusable method! In the template, we can call `add` with different sets of numbers, and it'll calculate the sum for us.

Important Note: Don't use arrow functions for methods. Why? Because Vue binds the `this` keyword to the data object within methods, and arrow functions don't have their own `this`. This means if you use an arrow function, `this` will become undefined inside the method, which can lead to errors.

Let's see an example:

```
<template>
  <div>
    <h2>{{ multiply(10) }}</h2>
  </div>
</template>

<script>
export default {
  data() {
    return {
      baseMultiplier: 5
    };
```

```
    },
    methods: {
      multiply(number) {
        // Using 'this' to access data property
        return number * this.baseMultiplier;
      }
    }
};
</script>
```

Here, we created a `baseMultiplier` data property and a `multiply` method that uses `this` to access it. This works perfectly.

Now, let's change `multiply` to an arrow function:

```
<template>
  <div>
    <h2>{{ multiply(10) }}</h2>
  </div>
</template>

<script>
export default {
  data() {
    return {
      baseMultiplier: 5
    };
  },
  methods: {
    multiply: (number) => {
      // 'this' is undefined here
      console.log(this)
      return number * this.baseMultiplier;
    }
  }
};
</script>
```

If we open this in the browser, we get an error: "Cannot read property 'baseMultiplier' of undefined." This is because `this` is undefined within an arrow function.

Remember: When creating methods, use regular functions, not arrow functions!

We also have a shortcut for accessing data properties within methods. Instead of using `this`, you can pass them in as arguments. For example:

```
<template>
```

```
  <div>
    <h2>{{ multiply(10, baseValue) }}</h2>
  </div>
</template>

<script>
export default {
  data() {
    return {
      baseMultiplier: 5,
      baseValue: 2
    };
  },
  methods: {
    multiply: (number, baseValue) => {
      return number * baseValue;
    }
  }
};
</script>
```

In this example, we pass `baseValue` as an argument to the `multiply` method, eliminating the need to use `this`.

Methods are a powerful tool in Vue. They help you organize your code, make it reusable, and improve maintainability. We'll see how methods play a critical role in event handling in the next chapter.

Event Handling

Imagine you're building a website. You want it to react when a user clicks a button, submits a form, or even just hovers their mouse over something. This is where event handling comes in! Vue makes it really easy to respond to user actions and make your web app interactive.

Let's start with a simple example. We'll create a new Vue component and bind a data property called "name" to our template. Then, we'll add a button that, when clicked, changes the value of "name."

```
<template>
  <div>
    <h1>{{ name }}</h1>
    <button v-on:click="changeName">Change Name</button>
  </div>
</template>

<script>
export default {
  data() {
    return {
      name: 'Developer'
    }
  },
  methods: {
    changeName() {
      this.name = 'Batman';
    }
  }
}
</script>
```

When you run this code, you'll see "Developer" displayed initially. Clicking the "Change Name" button will update the display to "Batman."

This is the core idea of event handling in Vue. We use the v-on directive (to listen for DOM events like click, mouseover, submit, and more. The value of the v-on directive can be:

- **Inline JavaScript:** Simple logic that runs directly within the directive itself.
- **Method name:** A reference to a method defined in the Vue component, allowing for more complex logic.

Let's look at another example to solidify this concept. We'll create a counter that can be incremented and decremented.

```
<template>
  <div>
    <h1>{{ count }}</h1>
    <button v-on:click="increment(5)">Increment +5</button>
    <button v-on:click="decrement(1)">Decrement -1</button>
  </div>
</template>

<script>
export default {
  data() {
    return {
      count: 0
    }
  },
  methods: {
    increment(num) {
      this.count += num;
    },
    decrement(num) {
      this.count -= num;
    }
  }
}
</script>
```

Here, we've added a `count` data property and two buttons. The buttons call the `increment` and `decrement` methods, respectively. The methods now take an optional `num` argument, allowing us to increment/decrement by different values.

This example demonstrates a couple of key points:

- **Method arguments:** You can pass arguments to methods called by `v-on`. This makes it flexible to control how much you want to increment or decrement the counter.
- **Reusable methods:** By using methods, we can easily reuse the same logic for multiple events or even different parts of our application.

So there you have it! That's the foundation of event handling in Vue. In the next section, we'll explore some more advanced techniques, so stay tuned!

Shorthand Syntax: @ Symbol

You've probably noticed that attaching event listeners is pretty common in web applications. Vue, being the awesome framework it is, provides a shorthand syntax for this using the "at" symbol (@).

Instead of writing `v-on:click` every time you want to bind an event, you can simply use `@click`. It's like a little shortcut for your fingers, saving you time and making your code cleaner.

Let's see this in action! Imagine we have a button that changes the name of someone.

```
<template>
  <button @click="changeName">Change Name</button>
</template>
```

This code snippet uses `@click` instead of `v-on:click` to bind the `changeName` method to the button's click event.

The Event Object: Accessing Event Details

Sometimes, you want to know more about the event itself. For example, where was the click on the screen? What type of event is it? Enter the **event object**!

Vue automatically passes the event object as an argument to your event handlers. Let's see how it works.

```
<template>
  <button @click="changeName">Change Name</button>
</template>

<script>
export default {
  data() {
    return {
      name: 'Developer'
    }
  },
  methods: {
    changeName(event) {
      console.log("Event:", event);
      this.name = "Batman";
    }
  }
};
</script>
```

In this example, we define a `changeName` method that takes an `event` argument. Inside the method, we log the `event` object to the console.

When you click the button, you'll see a lot of information in your browser's console. It tells you the type of event (click), the coordinates of the click, the target element, and much more. This information is super useful for customizing your application's behavior based on the event details.

Important Note: The event object is automatically passed only if you **don't** specify any other arguments to your event handler. If you have other arguments, like in a counter example where you pass a number to an increment method, Vue won't inject the event object. In those cases, you'll need to use a special variable called `$event` to access it.

```
<template>
  <button @click="increment(1, $event)">Increment 1</button>
</template>

<script>
export default {
  methods: {
    increment(amount, event) {
      console.log("Event:", event);
      // Your increment logic goes here
    }
  }
};
</script>
```

Multiple Event Handlers: Combining Actions

What if you want to trigger multiple actions when an event happens? Vue makes this easy! You can simply list the methods you want to call, separated by commas, within the `v-on` directive.

```
<template>
  <button @click="changeName, increment(1, $event)">Change
Name & Increment</button>
</template>
```

In this example, when you click the button, both `changeName` and `increment` methods will be called. Make sure to include `$event` if you need to access the event object in any of the methods!

Exercise

Create a simple counter that increments by 1 when a button is clicked. Use the event object to display the click coordinates in a separate element.

Solution:

```
<template>
  <div>
    <p>Count: {{ count }}</p>
    <button @click="increment($event)">Increment</button>
    <p>Click Coordinates: {{ clickX }}, {{ clickY }}</p>
  </div>
</template>

<script>
export default {
  data() {
    return {
      count: 0,
      clickX: 0,
      clickY: 0
    }
  },
  methods: {
    increment(event) {
      this.count++;
      this.clickX = event.clientX;
      this.clickY = event.clientY;
    }
  }
};
</script>
```

Form Handling

As a front-end developer, you know that building forms is a big part of the job. It's essential to understand how to capture user input using various form controls, like input fields, text areas, single and multi-select controls, checkboxes, and radio buttons. Once we capture this data, we also need to learn how to submit it. We'll focus on basic submission, like logging the data to the console, in this section.

We'll cover a lot of ground in this topic, so I've split it into two parts. This section will cover the basics of form handling and how to work with input fields, text areas, and single and multi-select controls. In the next section, we'll delve into checkboxes, radio buttons, and how to submit forms with a button click.

Form handling involves capturing data from the user and processing it based on your application's requirements. The form controls are placed in the `template` block, while their corresponding data resides in the `script` block. When a user fills out a form, we need a way to transfer this data to the `script` block. Similarly, if we have pre-existing data, like loading a saved form, we need a way to update the `template` block. The `template` and data need to remain in sync.

Thankfully, Vue provides the `v-model` directive to handle this scenario. It enables two-way binding, meaning it binds data from the `template` to the `script` and vice versa. This ensures your model and view are always in sync.

Now, let's jump into the code and understand the syntax and usage of the `v-model` directive. We'll create a simple job application form to illustrate the process.

Let's start by creating a simple form with a name field:

```
<template>
  <div>
    <pre>{{ JSON.stringify(formValues, null, 2) }}</pre>
    <form>
      <div>
        <label for="name">Name:</label>
        <input type="text" id="name" v-
model="formValues.name">
      </div>
```

```
      </form>
    </div>
  </template>
<script>
export default {
  data() {
    return {
      formValues: {
        name: '',
      }
    }
  }
}
</script>
```

In the `template` block, we have a `<form>` tag containing a `<div>` for our name field. The `<label>` tag with the `for` attribute links it to the `<input>` field. We use the `v-model` directive to bind the input field's value to the `name` property within the `formValues` object in the `script` block. Notice that we are also using a `<pre>` tag to display the `formValues` object as JSON in the browser, which will help us see how the data is being bound.

When you run this code, you'll see a form with a text input field labeled "Name". As you type in the field, the `name` property within the `formValues` object gets updated, and this updated value is reflected back in the input field. This demonstrates the two-way binding provided by `v-model`.

textarea

Let's add a text area field to capture the candidate's profile summary.

```
  <div>
    <label for="profile">Profile Summary:</label>
    <textarea id="profile" v-
model="formValues.profileSummary"></textarea>
  </div>
```

```
<script>
export default {
  data() {
    return {
      formValues: {
        // ...previous properties
        profileSummary: '',
```

```
          }
        }
      }
    }
  }
</script>
```

Here, we've added a new `<div>` containing a `<label>` and a `<textarea>` element. We've created a new `profileSummary` property in the `formValues` object and bound it to the `textarea` using `v-model`.

input

Add a new data property called `email` to the `formValues` object and a corresponding `<input>` field in the template. Bind this new property to the input using `v-model`.

```
<script>
export default {
  data() {
    return {
      formValues: {
        // ...previous properties
        email: '',
      }
    }
  }
}
</script>
  <div>
    <label for="email">Email:</label>
    <input type="email" id="email" v-
model="formValues.email">
  </div>
```

dropdown

Next, we'll add a dropdown to capture the user's country.

```
  <div>
    <label for="country">Country:</label>
    <select id="country" v-model="formValues.country">
      <option value="">Select a Country</option>
      <option value="USA">USA</option>
      <option value="UK">UK</option>
      <option value="Singapore">Singapore</option>
```

```
      </select>
    </div>


<script>
export default {
  data() {
    return {
      formValues: {
        // ...previous properties
        country: ''
      }
    }
  }
}
</script>
```

We've created a new `<div>` containing a `<label>` and a `<select>` element. We've added a `country` property in the `formValues` object and bound it to the `select` element using `v-model`. The `<option>` tags within the `<select>` element define the available choices for the dropdown.

Multi-Select Dropdown

Lastly, we'll add a multi-select dropdown to capture the user's preferred relocation locations.

```
    <div>
      <label for="job-location">Job Location:</label>
      <select id="job-location" v-
model="formValues.jobLocation" multiple>
        <option value="USA">USA</option>
        <option value="UK">UK</option>
        <option value="Singapore">Singapore</option>
      </select>
    </div>

<script>
export default {
  data() {
    return {
      formValues: {
        // ...previous properties
        jobLocation: [] ,
      }
    }
  }
}
```

```
</script>
```

We've created a new `<div>` containing a `<label>` and a `<select>` element. We've added a `jobLocation` property, initialized as an empty array, to the `formValues` object and bound it to the `select` element using `v-model`. The `multiple` attribute on the `<select>` tag allows users to select multiple options.

We've covered a lot in this section! We've learned about the basics of form handling in Vue, and how to use the `v-model` directive to achieve two-way binding between our data and the form controls. We've also looked at various form control types, including input fields, text areas, single and multi-select dropdowns.

checkbox

In our job applicant form, we want the user to tell us if they're okay with working remotely. Like other form controls, we can implement this in three simple steps.

Step 1: Add a new data property called `remoteWork` and initialize it to `false`. A single checkbox usually indicates true or false, so we start with `false` so the checkbox is initially unchecked.

Step 2: Add the HTML. In our template, we'll add another `div` tag. Inside the `div` tag, we start with the `input` element. We set the `type` to `checkbox` and the `id` to `remoteWork`. Next, we add a `label` with `for="remoteWork"` and the text "Open to remote work?". That's our step two.

Step 3: Bind the `remoteWork` data property using the `v-model` directive. We'll set `v-model="formValues.remoteWork"`.

```
<template>
  <div>
    <!-- ... Previous form elements ... -->
    <div>
      <input type="checkbox" id="remoteWork" v-model="formValues.remoteWork" />
      <label for="remoteWork">Open to remote work?</label>
    </div>
  </div>
</template>

<script>
export default {
```

```
data() {
  return {
    formValues: {
      // ...previous properties
      remoteWork: false ,
    }
  }
}
}
</script>
```

Now, if you save the file and look at your browser, you'll see the checkbox. In the `formValues` object, you'll see the initial value is `false`. When you check the box, the value becomes `true`. The `v-model` directive keeps the data property and the checkbox in sync.

This works well for most scenarios, but sometimes you don't want boolean values. Instead, you might want something like "yes" or "no" stored in your database. We can achieve this using the `true-value` and `false-value` attributes.

```
<template>
  <div>
    <!-- ... Previous form elements ... -->
    <div>
      <input
        type="checkbox"
        id="remoteWork"
        v-model="formValues.remoteWork"
        :true-value="'yes'"
        :false-value="'no'"
      />
      <label for="remoteWork">Open to remote work?</label>
    </div>
  </div>
</template>
```

If we set the initial value of `remoteWork` to "no", then our checkbox will display "no" initially. When checked, the value will change to "yes". This lets you control the values assigned for the checked and unchecked states of a checkbox.

Multiple checkbox

Now, let's understand how to work with multiple checkboxes, or a checkbox group. In our job applicant form, we want the user to select from a list of skills they're comfortable with. Let's use HTML, CSS, and JavaScript as our checkboxes. The user can select more than one skill.

Step 1: Add a new data property called `skillset` and initialize it to an empty array. We'll use an array because the user can select multiple values.

Step 2: Add the HTML. To save time, we'll copy and paste the HTML and then go through the code.

Step 3: We'll bind the `skillset` data property using the `v-model` directive on each checkbox. The `v-model` is set to `formValues.skillset` for all three checkboxes.

```
<template>
  <div>
    <!-- ... Previous form elements ... -->
    <div>
      <label for="skillset">Skillset</label>
      <div>
        <input
          type="checkbox"
          id="html"
          value="html"
          v-model="formValues.skillset"
        />
        <label for="html">HTML</label>
      </div>
      <div>
        <input
          type="checkbox"
          id="css"
          value="css"
          v-model="formValues.skillset"
        />
        <label for="css">CSS</label>
      </div>
      <div>
        <input
          type="checkbox"
          id="javascript"
          value="javascript"
          v-model="formValues.skillset"
        />
        <label for="javascript">JavaScript</label>
      </div>
    </div>
  </div>
</template>
```

We have a `div` for the checkbox group and a `label` for "Skillset". Then, we have three checkboxes: one for HTML, one for CSS, and one for JavaScript. Each checkbox has a `value` that matches its `id` and `for` attributes.

```
<script>
export default {
  data() {
    return {
      formValues: {
        // ...previous properties
        skillSet: [] ,
      }
    }
  }
}
</script>
```

Now, save the file and check your browser. You'll see the three checkboxes for the skillset input. The `skillset` property in the `formValues` object is an empty array. When you select HTML, the value "html" is pushed to the array. If you select all three, all three values will be pushed to the array. Our checkbox group works as expected.

Let's look at the final form control, the radio group. Let's say we need the job applicant to select their years of experience. They can choose from: 0-2 years, 3-5 years, 6-10 years, or 10+ years. The user can only select one option, making the radio group the best choice.

Step 1: Create a data property called `yearsOfExperience` and initialize it to an empty string.

Step 2: Add the HTML. The HTML is similar to the checkbox group, so we'll copy and paste it and walk through the code.

```
<template>
  <div>
    <!-- ... Previous form elements ... -->
    <div>
      <label for="yearsOfExperience">Years of
Experience</label>
      <div>
        <input
          type="radio"
          id="0-2"
          value="0-2"
          v-model="formValues.yearsOfExperience"
```

```
      />
      <label for="0-2">0-2 years</label>
    </div>
    <div>
      <input
        type="radio"
        id="3-5"
        value="3-5"
        v-model="formValues.yearsOfExperience"
      />
      <label for="3-5">3-5 years</label>
    </div>
    <div>
      <input
        type="radio"
        id="6-10"
        value="6-10"
        v-model="formValues.yearsOfExperience"
      />
      <label for="6-10">6-10 years</label>
    </div>
    <div>
      <input
        type="radio"
        id="10+"
        value="10+"
        v-model="formValues.yearsOfExperience"
      />
      <label for="10+">10+ years</label>
    </div>
  </div>
 </div>
</template>
```

We have a div tag and a label for "Years of Experience". Then, we have four radio buttons, each with a label and an input of type radio. Each radio button has a unique id, value, and for attribute. We've also included the v-model directive, which is our step three.

Step 3: The v-model is bound to the yearsOfExperience property.

```
<script>
export default {
  data() {
    return {
      formValues: {
        // ...previous properties
        yearsOfExperience: '',
```

```
      }
    }
  }
}
</script>
```

Save the file and go to your browser. You'll see the four radio buttons. The initial value in the `formValues` object is an empty string. When you select a radio button, its corresponding value is reflected in the `formValues` object. Our radio group control works as expected.

Now that we understand how to work with different form controls, let's learn how to submit this form data.

First, we'll add a submit button to our form. After the radio group control, add another `div` tag and then a button with the text "Submit".

```
<template>
  <div>
    <!-- ... Previous form elements ... -->
    <div>
      <button type="submit">Submit</button>
    </div>
  </div>
</template>
```

When the submit button is clicked, the form emits a `submit` event. We can listen for this event using event binding. We'll bind to the `submit` event on the form tag and assign an event handler called `submitForm`.

```
<template>
  <form @submit="submitForm">
    <!-- ... form elements ... -->
    <div>
      <button type="submit">Submit</button>
    </div>
  </form>
</template>
```

The `submitForm` will be a method, so let's define it in the `methods` object in our script block. The `submitForm` method receives the event argument by default.

A form submission normally causes the page to refresh. To prevent this, we'll call `event.preventDefault()`. In the next line, we'll log the `formValues` object to the console.

```
<script>
export default {
```

```
  data() {
    return {
      formValues: {
        // ...previous properties
      }
    }
  } ,

  methods: {
    submitForm(event) {
      event.preventDefault();
      console.log(this.formValues);
    },
  },
};
</script>
```

In a real application, you would usually send this object to an API endpoint as the request body. For now, we just want to understand how to get hold of the form data when the submit button is clicked.

Save the file, go to the browser, open the console dev tools, fill in all the form values, and click on "Submit". You'll see the `formValues` object logged to the console, containing all the values you entered.

That covers the fundamentals of form handling in Vue. You now have a good understanding of the `v-model` directive, how to capture values from various form controls, and how to submit form data entered by the user.

Modifiers

In this section, we're diving into modifiers in Vue. Think of modifiers as little helpers you can add to directives like `v-on` and `v-model` to add extra functionality directly within your template. It's one of those neat things Vue offers to keep your code clean and tidy!

Let's start with the **trim modifier**. Imagine you're building a form and you want to automatically remove any extra spaces (like those pesky spaces at the beginning or end of a word) from a user's input. This is where the trim modifier comes in handy!

To see this in action, let's look at our job applicant form. If you type in the "name" field with spaces before and after your name, you'll see those spaces show up in the `formValues` object. That's because JavaScript doesn't automatically trim whitespace. But with the `trim` modifier, we can fix that!

```
<template>
  <div>
    <label for="name">Name:</label>
    <input type="text" id="name" v-
model.trim="formValues.name" />
  </div>
</template>
```

In your `v-model` directive, just add `.trim` as a suffix like this: `v-model.trim`. Now, when you type in the "name" field and save your code, refresh your browser, and give it a try. Type some spaces before and after your name – you'll see those spaces disappear!

The Number Modifier

Next up is the **number modifier**, which makes sure your input is stored as a number, not a string. Let's say we want the job applicant to enter their age. We can add an input field for that:

```
<template>
  <div>
    <label for="age">Age:</label>
    <input type="number" id="age" v-
model.number="formValues.age" />
  </div>
</template>
```

Notice we're using an `input` of type "number." But if you save the code, refresh the page, and enter an age, you'll see that it's stored as a string in the `formValues` object. This is because of how JavaScript handles input types. However, we can force it to be a number by using the `number` modifier! Add `.number` to the end of your `v-model` directive. Now, try entering a number again. Notice the difference? The value is stored as a number, not a string. That's the power of the number modifier.

The Lazy Modifier

The **lazy modifier** changes when the value in your `v-model` is updated. Normally, every time you type a character, the value is immediately updated. This can be helpful if you want to see the changes live, but often you only need to update the value when the input field loses focus (when you click outside the input).

To use the `lazy` modifier, add `.lazy` to your `v-model` directive. Let's add it to our name field. Remember, we can chain modifiers!

```
<template>
  <div>
    <label for="name">Name:</label>
    <input type="text" id="name" v-
model.trim.lazy="formValues.name" />
  </div>
</template>
```

Now, type in the "name" field. Notice that the `formValues` object only updates when you click outside the field. The `lazy` modifier is great for performance because it doesn't update with every keystroke.

The Prevent Modifier

Let's talk about the **prevent modifier**. It's basically the same as calling `event.preventDefault()` in a method.

Remember how we used `event.preventDefault()` in our `submitForm` method to stop the page from refreshing when the form was submitted?

```
submitForm(event) {
  event.preventDefault();
  // do something else
}
```

We can replace that with the `prevent` modifier directly in our template!

```
<template>
  <form @submit.prevent="submitForm">
    <!-- Form content goes here -->
  </form>
</template>
```

Now, the submitForm method is called, and the form doesn't refresh. This is a clean way to keep your form submission logic in your template and avoid writing extra code.

The Key Modifier

The **key modifier** lets you trigger a method when a specific key is pressed. Let's say we want to submit our form when the user presses the "Enter" key in the "age" field.

First, let's remove the submit button from our template. Now, we'll add a key up event listener to the "age" field, and use the enter modifier:

```
<template>
  <div>
    <label for="age">Age:</label>
    <input type="number" id="age" v-
model.number="formValues.age" @keyup.enter="submitForm" />
  </div>
</template>
```

Now, if you type in the "age" field and press "Enter", the submitForm method is called, and the form is submitted!

There are plenty of other key modifiers you can use, such as tab, delete, escape, space, arrow keys, ctrl, alt, and shift. You can even use mouse modifiers like left, right, and middle. Explore these modifiers based on your specific needs.

And that's it for modifiers in Vue! Keep experimenting and you'll find them incredibly useful in building interactive and user-friendly applications.

Directives

In this section, we're diving into two special directives offered by Vue.js that you might come across in some projects, but aren't used as often: v-once and v-pre.

The *v-once* Directive: Rendering Once and For All

Think of v-once as a way to tell Vue, "Hey, I only want this part of the template to be rendered once. Don't touch it again, no matter what happens." This comes in handy when you have a big chunk of content that you know will never change, like a website's copyright notice or a static header. By using v-once, Vue can skip checking this content during updates, which can speed things up.

Let's see it in action! We'll start with a simple example:

```
<template>
  <div>
    <h2 v-once>My name is: {{ name }}</h2>
    <button @click="changeName">Change Name</button>
  </div>
</template>

<script>
export default {
  data() {
    return {
      name: "Developer",
    };
  },
  methods: {
    changeName() {
      this.name = "Batman";
    },
  },
};
</script>
```

Here, we have an h2 tag displaying a name and a button to change it. If you add the v-once directive to the h2 tag, the name will only update once, and subsequent changes will be ignored.

The `v-pre` *Directive: Skipping Compilation*

Now, let's talk about `v-pre`. Imagine you have some HTML that contains double curly braces (`{{ }}`) but you don't want Vue to treat them as data bindings. You want the text inside those braces to appear exactly as it is. That's where `v-pre` steps in. It instructs Vue to skip compiling the HTML inside the element it's attached to.

Let's say we want to display the text "{{ name }}" literally, without Vue trying to replace it with the value of the `name` property. Here's how we'd use `v-pre`:

```
<template>
  <div>
    <h2 v-pre>My name is: {{ name }}</h2>
  </div>
</template>

<script>
export default {
  data() {
    return {
      name: "Developer",
    };
  },
};
</script>
```

In this case, the `h2` tag will display "My name is: {{ name }}" as plain text, because the `v-pre` directive tells Vue to treat the content as raw HTML.

Exercise: Try it Out!

Let's put these directives to the test.

- **Create a new Vue component.**
- **Add a data property named** `message` **with the value "Hello, world!"**
- **Use the** v-once **directive on an** h1 **element to display the** message **property.**
- **Add a button that, when clicked, changes the** message **property to "Goodbye, world!".**
- **Notice how the** h1 **element only changes once, despite multiple clicks.**
- **Now, add a paragraph element with the text "This is a**

{{ message }}" and use the `v-pre` **directive on it. Observe how the double curly braces are displayed as text.**

While `v-once` and `v-pre` are useful in certain situations, you'll likely encounter them less often than other directives. They are handy for fine-tuning performance and controlling how Vue interacts with your HTML.

Computed Properties

In this section, we're diving into **computed properties** in Vue.js. You've already learned some cool ways to display data in your user interface. You can use static HTML, bind data properties with text interpolation, write simple expressions in the mustache syntax, and even call methods to get values for your UI.

Computed properties add another powerful tool to your toolkit. Let's break it down. Imagine you need to create a new piece of data from other existing information. You could do this by directly manipulating your data in your template, but that can lead to messy code that's hard to maintain. That's where computed properties shine!

Computed properties are like smart data properties. They let you combine or manipulate existing data and present it in a new way. The best part? They're super efficient because they act like **cached calculations.** They only update when the data they depend on changes, saving you precious processing power.

Let's see this in action!

```
<template>
  <h2>Full Name: {{ fullName }}</h2>
</template>

<script>
export default {
  data() {
    return {
      firstName: 'Bruce',
      lastName: 'Wayne',
    };
  },
  computed: {
    fullName() {
      return `${this.firstName} ${this.lastName}`;
    },
  },
};
</script>
```

Here's what's happening:

- We have two data properties: firstName and lastName.

- We define a computed property named `fullName`.
- Inside the `fullName` function, we combine `firstName` and `lastName` to create a full name.
- In the template, we use the mustache syntax to display the `fullName` computed property.

The output will be:

```
Full Name: David Stone
```

But why bother with a computed property when you could just use text interpolation directly in the template?

```
<h2>Full Name: {{ firstName }} {{ lastName }}</h2>
```

Both approaches achieve the same result, but there are some key differences:

- **Readability:** `fullName` is more descriptive of what it represents than simply combining `firstName` and `lastName` in the template.
- **Reusability:** If you need to display the full name in multiple places, using a computed property makes your code much cleaner and easier to maintain.

Let's look at another example:

```
<template>
  <h2>Total: {{ total }}</h2>
</template>

<script>
export default {
  data() {
    return {
      items: [
        { id: 1, title: 'TV', price: 400 },
        { id: 2, title: 'Phone', price: 200 },
        { id: 3, title: 'Laptop', price: 300 },
      ],
    };
  },
  computed: {
    total() {
      return this.items.reduce((total, item) => total +
item.price, 0);
    },
  },
};
</script>
```

We have an array of items, and we need to calculate the total cost.

Using a computed property, we define `total` and use the `reduce` method to sum up the prices of all the items.

The output will be:

```
Total: 900
```

Imagine you need to display the total in your shopping cart icon and also in the order summary. Without a computed property, you'd have to repeat the same code in both places. Now, you only have to update the `total` computed property, and it automatically updates everywhere it's used!

But wait, there's more!

Let's add a button to add a new item to the `items` array:

```
<template>
  <button @click="addItem">Add Item</button>
</template>

<script>
export default {
  // ... (data and computed properties from previous
example)
  methods: {
    addItem() {
      this.items.push({ id: 4, title: 'Keyboard', price:
50 });
    },
  },
};
</script>
```

Now, when you click the button, a new item is added to the `items` array. **Guess what? The `total` computed property automatically recalculates, and the updated total is displayed on the screen!**

This magic happens because Vue.js intelligently tracks dependencies. Whenever a computed property's dependencies change, it automatically re-evaluates itself.

You don't have to worry about manually updating your computed properties. Vue takes care of everything for you.

Now, you might be thinking, "Can't I just use a method to do this logic instead?"

Yes, you technically could, but computed properties are often a better choice because of their efficiency and the way they integrate seamlessly with Vue's reactivity system.

Computed Properties vs Methods

We have learned all about computed properties, their uses, and why they're a better choice than data properties in certain scenarios. We even saw an example where we calculated the total price of items in an array using a computed property. We also learned how computed properties are recalculated whenever their dependencies change.

But remember, we had a question at the end: **Can't we calculate the total using a method and then call it in our template? Why use a computed property at all?** Let's figure that out by creating an example.

Since we already have a computed property called "total" for displaying the total price, let's create a method that does the same thing. In our methods object, let's define a new function called getTotal. This function will return the same value as our computed property. Copy and paste the code from our computed property into the getTotal function.

```
methods: {
  getTotal() {
    return this.items.reduce((total, item) => total +
item.price, 0);
  }
}
```

Now, let's bind it to our template h2 tag where we display the total:

```
<h2 v-if="items.length">Total: {{ getTotal() }}</h2>
```

If you save the file and refresh your browser, you'll see the total displayed using our getTotal method. If we click the "Add Item" button, you'll see that both the computed property value and the getTotal method value update. So, what's the difference?

The main difference lies in **caching**. Computed properties are cached! This means if something unrelated to the computed property changes on the page, and the UI re-renders, the cached result will be returned, and the computed property will not be recalculated. This boosts performance by avoiding potentially expensive operations.

Let's understand this with a new example. Let's add a text field and bind its data to a property. We'll create a new data property called `country`:

```
data() {
  return {
    // ... existing data properties
    country: ''
  }
}
```

Now, let's add an input element in our template and bind it to the `country` property using `v-model`:

```
<input type="text" v-model="country">
```

Finally, let's add `console.log` statements to both our `getTotal` method and our computed property:

```
methods: {
  getTotal() {
    console.log('get total method');
    return this.items.reduce((total, item) => total +
item.price, 0);
  }
}

computed: {
  total() {
    console.log('total computed property');
    return this.items.reduce((total, item) => total +
item.price, 0);
  }
}
```

Save the file and go back to the browser. You'll see the log statements from both the method and the computed property when the page loads.

Now, click the "Add Item" button. Again, both the logs appear. The method is run, and the computed property recalculates to update the UI.

Let's get to the interesting part. Focus on the `country` text field. Type a letter in the text field. You'll see that the `getTotal` method is called, but the computed property doesn't recalculate.

If you keep typing, for example, "United," which has six letters, you'll see the `getTotal` method is called six times, while the computed property remains unchanged.

This is the key difference:

- **Computed Properties** use caching. If something in the UI changes that

doesn't affect the computed property's dependencies, Vue will reuse the already computed value instead of recalculating it.
- **Methods** are always called whenever there's a change in the UI, regardless of whether the change affects their logic or not.

So, if you have a computationally heavy operation, a computed property is the better choice for performance.

Computed Properties and v-for

Remember those list rendering sections we covered a while back? We even learned how to use v-if to add some conditional filtering to our lists. Let's refresh our memory with a quick example. Imagine you have an array of items, and you want to display only the "expensive" ones. We'll consider an item expensive if its price is above 100.

We could achieve this using v-for and v-if combined with a template tag. Let's get our hands dirty and write some code.

```
<template>
  <div>
    <template v-for="item in items" :key="item.id">
      <h2 v-if="item.price > 100">
        {{ item.title }} - ${{ item.price }}
      </h2>
    </template>
  </div>
</template>

<script>
export default {
  data() {
    return {
      items: [
        { id: 1, title: 'Phone', price: 200 },
        { id: 2, title: 'Laptop', price: 150 },
        { id: 3, title: 'Keyboard', price: 75 },
        { id: 4, title: 'Mouse', price: 25 },
      ],
    };
  },
};
</script>
```

Here, we're iterating through the items array using v-for. The v-if directive ensures that we only render the h2 tag for items where the price is greater than 100.

Now, if you run this code, you'll see that "Phone" and "Laptop" are displayed because their prices are above 100. But hold on! There's a better way to do this using computed properties.

Let's rewrite our code to use a computed property called `expensiveItems`.

```
<template>
  <div>
    <template v-for="item in expensiveItems" :key="item.id">
      <h2>
        {{ item.title }} - ${{ item.price }}
      </h2>
    </template>
  </div>
</template>

<script>
export default {
  data() {
    return {
      items: [
        { id: 1, title: 'Phone', price: 50 },
        { id: 2, title: 'Laptop', price: 150 },
        { id: 3, title: 'Keyboard', price: 75 },
        { id: 4, title: 'Mouse', price: 25 },
      ],
    };
  },
  computed: {
    expensiveItems() {
      return this.items.filter(item => item.price > 100);
    },
  },
};
</script>
```

Inside our computed property, `expensiveItems`, we use the `filter` method to create a new array containing only items with a price greater than 100. Now, instead of using `v-if` in our template, we simply iterate through `expensiveItems` using `v-for`.

The magic here is that Vue.js will automatically update the `expensiveItems` array whenever the `items` array changes. So, if you add or remove items, or change their prices, the `expensiveItems` array will be recalculated. This is where the power of computed properties shines!

Why is this better than the previous approach? Computed properties are **cached**. This means that Vue.js will only recalculate the `expensiveItems` array when something in the `items` array changes. This avoids unnecessary re-calculations, making your application more performant.

Imagine you have a large table with lots of data that needs to be sorted or filtered. Using computed properties for your sorting or filtering logic can dramatically improve the responsiveness of your app.

Computed Setter

Imagine you're making an API call and storing the result in a computed property. You might want to allow the user to edit that data and then send it back to the server. Let's see how to do that using the power of getters and setters!

Getters and Setters

We'll go back to our trusty `fullName` example. Remember, we had `firstName` and `lastName` data properties, and a computed property `fullName` that combined them.

```
<template>
  <div >
    <p>Full Name: {{ fullName }}</p>
    <button @click="changeFullName">Change Full
Name</button>
  </div>
</template>

<script>
export default {
  data() {
    return {
      firstName: 'Bruce',
      lastName: 'Wayne',
    };
  },
  computed: {
    fullName: {
      get() {
        return this.firstName + ' ' + this.lastName;
      },
      set(newValue) {
        const names = newValue.split(' ');
        this.firstName = names[0];
```

```
          this.lastName = names[1];
        }
      }
    },
    methods: {
      changeFullName() {
        this.fullName = 'Clark Kent';
      }
    }
};
</script>
```

Instead of just a function, we now have an object for `fullName` with a `get` and `set` property.

- `get:` This is the familiar function that gets called whenever you read the `fullName` property. It returns the combined first and last name.
- `set:` This is the new guy! It gets called whenever you *assign* a new value to `fullName`. It takes the new value (like "Clark Kent") and splits it into two parts based on the space. Then, it updates our `firstName` and `lastName` data properties to keep everything in sync.

Head to your browser and see the magic in action. You'll initially see "David Stone" as the full name. Click the "Change Full Name" button and watch it transform to "Clark Kent". Our getter and setter functions are working seamlessly, ensuring both our data properties and computed property stay in sync!

Remember: Computed setters are a powerful tool for creating dynamic, two-way communication between your computed properties and the underlying data. It's like having a magic bridge for updating information in a controlled and organized way.

Exercise:

Modify the example to include a third data property, `middleName`. Update the `fullName` computed property to include the `middleName`. Also, update the `set` function to handle situations where the user might enter a full name with a middle name.

Solution:

```
computed: {
  fullName: {
    get() {
      return this.firstName + ' ' + this.middleName + ' ' +
this.lastName;
```

```
  },
  set(newValue) {
    const names = newValue.split(' ');
    this.firstName = names[0];
    this.middleName = names[1];
    this.lastName = names[2];
  }
 }
}
```

Watchers

In this section, we're going to dive into the world of watchers in Vue. Watchers, as the name suggests, allow you to keep an eye on any data property or computed property in your application and run some code whenever their values change.

Let's get our hands dirty with a simple example. We'll build a volume tracker. Imagine you're creating a music player and need to show the current volume and let the user increase or decrease it.

First, let's set up the basic structure. We'll have an h2 tag for the title "Volume Tracker" and an h3 tag to display the current volume. We'll also add two buttons – one to increase the volume and another to decrease it.

```
<template>
  <h2>Volume Tracker (0 to 20)</h2>
  <h3>Current volume: {{ volume }}</h3>
  <div>
    <button @click="volume += 2">Increase</button>
    <button @click="volume -= 2">Decrease</button>
  </div>
</template>

<script>
export default {
  data() {
    return {
      volume: 0,
    };
  },
};
</script>
```

This code defines a volume property in our data object and uses it to display the current volume in the h3 tag. Clicking the buttons will increment or decrement the volume by two.

Now, let's say our client wants an alert to pop up when the volume reaches 20. This is where watchers come in!

We can define a watch property in our component's script block. This property is an object where each key represents the data or computed property we want to watch, and the value is a function that will be executed whenever the property's value changes.

```
export default {
  data() {
    return {
      volume: 0,
    };
  },
  watch: {
    volume(newValue, oldValue) {
      if (newValue > oldValue && newValue === 20) {
        alert("Listening to a high volume for a long time
may damage your hearing.");
      }
    },
  },
};
```

In this example, we watch the `volume` property. When it changes, the function is executed with the new value (`newValue`) and the old value (`oldValue`) as arguments. We then check if the volume has increased to 20. If it has, we display the alert message.

Now, let's see this in action! When you run the code, you'll notice that the alert only appears when you increase the volume from 19 to 20. Decreasing the volume to 20 won't trigger the alert because the `newValue > oldValue` condition is not met.

So, what's the big picture here? Watchers are incredibly versatile. They can help you handle complex data interactions, perform actions based on changes in your data, or even trigger API calls in response to data updates.

But remember, there's a time and a place for everything. Watchers provide a flexible way to react to data changes, but for simple data transformations, computed properties are often a cleaner and more efficient choice.

Here's a quick recap of when to choose computed properties and when to go with watchers:

- **Computed properties:** Use them when you need to derive new data from existing data sources or simplify access to deeply nested properties.
- **Watchers:** Use them when you need to perform specific actions in response to data changes, like triggering API calls or implementing UI updates based on specific data conditions.

Exercise:

Create a simple counter application that displays the current count. Implement a watcher that increments the count by 1 every 2 seconds.

Solution:

```
<template>
  <div>
    <h1>Counter: {{ count }}</h1>
    <button @click="incrementCount">Increment</button>
  </div>
</template>

<script>
export default {
  data() {
    return {
      count: 0,
    };
  },
  methods: {
    incrementCount() {
      this.count++;
    },
  },
  watch: {
    count(newValue) {
      setTimeout(() => {
        this.count = newValue + 1;
      }, 2000);
    },
  },
};
</script>
```

In this example, the count watcher is triggered whenever the count value changes. Inside the watcher, we use setTimeout to increment the count by 1 after a delay of 2 seconds.

That's it, folks! In the next section, we'll explore more advanced features of watchers and delve deeper into their potential applications.

Immediate and Deep Watchers

In the last section, we learned about watchers in Vue. Now, we're diving a little deeper into them to make sure you've got a solid grasp.

Imagine you have a movie app, and you want to update your movie list whenever a user types in a new movie title. We'll set up a watcher to handle this.

First, let's create a data property called `movie` and set it to an empty string. In our template, we'll add an input element and bind it to the `movie` property using the `v-model` directive:

```
<template>
  <div>
    <input type="text" v-model="movie" />
  </div>
</template>

<script>
export default {
  data() {
    return {
      movie: '',
    };
  },
};
</script>
```

Now, let's create a watcher for the `movie` property:

```
<script>
export default {
  // ...
  watch: {
    movie(newValue) {
      console.log(`Calling API with movie name: $
{newValue}`);
    },
  },
};
</script>
```

This watcher will execute whenever the value of `movie` changes. If we type "Batman" in the input field, we'll see the following output in the console:

```
Calling API with movie name: Batman
```

This works great, but what if we want to call the API when the page loads, even if the `movie` value is an empty string? That's where the `immediate` property comes in.

Let's change our watcher slightly:

```
<script>
```

```
export default {
  // ...
  watch: {
    movie: {
      handler(newValue) {
        console.log(`Calling API with movie name: $
{newValue}`);
      },
      immediate: true,
    },
  },
};
</script>
```

By setting `immediate` to `true`, we tell Vue to run the watcher function right when the page loads. Now, we'll see the output in the console even before typing anything in the input:

```
Calling API with movie name:
```

So, that's the `immediate` property – it runs the watcher once at the beginning.

Now, let's talk about the `deep` property. This one is handy when working with objects and arrays.

Let's create a new data property called `movieInfo`, which is an object with two properties: `title` and `actor`:

```
<script>
export default {
  data() {
    return {
      // ...
      movieInfo: {
        title: '',
        actor: '',
      },
    };
  },
};
</script>
```

In our template, we'll add two more input elements, one for the `title` and one for the `actor`:

```
<template>
  <div>
    <input type="text" v-model="movieInfo.title" />
    <input type="text" v-model="movieInfo.actor" />
```

```
    </div>
</template>
```

Now, let's create a watcher for the `movieInfo` object:

```
<script>
export default {
  // ...
  watch: {
    movie: {
      handler(newValue) {
        console.log(`Calling API with movie name: $
{newValue}`);
      },
      immediate: true,
    },
    movieInfo(newValue) {
      console.log(`Calling API with movie title: $
{newValue.title}, actor: ${newValue.actor}`);
    },
  },
};
</script>
```

But here's the catch – if we start typing in the input fields, we won't see anything in the console. That's because, by default, watchers don't watch for changes inside objects. To fix this, we need to use the `deep` property:

```
<script>
export default {
  // ...
  watch: {
    // ...
    movieInfo: {
      handler(newValue) {
        console.log(`Calling API with movie title: $
{newValue.title}, actor: ${newValue.actor}`);
      },
      deep: true,
    },
  },
};
</script>
```

With `deep: true`, Vue will now watch for changes within the `movieInfo` object. Now, when we type in the input fields, we'll see the output in the console as we update the properties.

The `deep` property is also useful when working with arrays. Let's say we have a data property called `movieList`, which is an array of movie titles:

```
<script>
export default {
  data() {
    return {
      // ...
      movieList: ['Batman', 'Superman'],
    };
  },
};
</script>
```

In our template, we'll add a button that pushes a new movie title into the `movieList` array:

```
<template>
  <div>
    <button @click="movieList.push('Wonder Woman')">Add
Movie</button>
  </div>
</template>
```

Let's create a watcher for the `movieList` array:

```
<script>
export default {
  // ...
  watch: {
    // ...
    movieList(newValue) {
      console.log(`Updated movie list: ${newValue}`);
    },
  },
};
</script>
```

If we click the button, we won't see the updated movie list in the console. That's because, by default, watchers don't watch for changes within arrays either. We need the `deep` property:

```
<script>
export default {
  // ...
  watch: {
    // ...
    movieList: {
      handler(newValue) {
        console.log(`Updated movie list: ${newValue}`);
      },
      deep: true,
    },
  },
```

```
};
</script>
```

Now, when we click the button, we'll see the updated list in the console:

```
Updated movie list: ["Batman", "Superman", "Wonder Woman"]
```

It's important to remember that if you return a new reference (like with `Array.concat`) instead of modifying the existing object or array, the `deep` property is not necessary.

So, those are the `immediate` and `deep` properties – they give you more control over how watchers behave.

Components

Now that we have a good understanding of the fundamental concepts in Vue, it's time to dive into the component architecture. Components are crucial for building medium to large-scale enterprise applications, just like in React and Angular.

Vue follows a component-based architecture, which means you break down your application into small, self-contained units called components. These components can then be combined to create more complex user interfaces. Imagine a traditional website with a header, side navigation, main content area, and footer. This website could be built with five components: one for the header, one for the side navigation, one for the main content, one for the footer, and one overarching component to hold everything together. This overarching component is called the root component and is usually named "App", residing in a file called `App.vue` in your project.

Each of the nested components represents a specific part of the UI. Although they are separate entities, they work together to form the entire application. Components are also reusable, meaning you can use the same component with different properties to display different information. For example, a side navigation component could be used for both the left and right sides of your application, with only the data changing.

So how does this component concept translate into code? We've already seen a glimpse of it. A component's code typically lives in a `.vue` file and contains three parts: a template block, a script block, and a style block. `App.vue` is a prime example. In real-world applications, you might create dozens or even hundreds of components, each representing a specific portion of the UI.

Create 'components' folder because we deleted it earlier, if you did as well. Now, let's create our very first component. It will simply display the text "Hello Developer" in the browser. In the `components` folder, which was automatically generated, create a new file named `greet.vue`. This component needs to render that text, so we'll use an HTML template. Add a `<template>` tag and an `<h2>` tag inside, containing "Hello Developer".

```
<template>
  <h2>Hello Developer</h2>
```

```
</template>
```

We now have the HTML to render, but it won't show up in the browser yet. Why? Because our `greet` component is not connected to the rest of our application. To make this happen, we need to export the `greet` component from `GreetUser.vue`, import it into `App.vue`, and then include it in the `App` component's template. In other words, we need to register the `greet` component with our application.

Let's start with exporting the `greetuser` component. After the `<template>` tag, add a `<script>` tag. Inside this tag, we use a default export to create an object with a property called `name`, which is the name of the component. We'll name it `Greet`. The name export is optional, but your conponent name must be multi-world, such as `GreetUser.vue`. It is a good practice to always use multi-word either way. Try to read the naming convention here link .

```
<script>
export default {
  name: 'GreetUser'
}
</script>
```

Now, let's import this component into `App.vue`. In `App.vue`, within the `<script>` block, import the `greet` component using the relative path to its location:

```
<script>
import GreetUser from './components/GreetUser.vue'
// ...rest of your code
</script>
```

Finally, to include the `greet` component in our `App` component, we'll add a custom HTML tag within the `App` component's template. If there's no content between the tags, you can use a self-closing tag.

```
<template>
  <GreetUser/>
</template>
```

However, the `App` component doesn't recognize `greet` yet. So, we need to specify a `components` property in the `App` component's `<script>` block, listing the `greet` component with its corresponding name as both the key and value. We can use the shorthand syntax in ES6.

```
<script>
import GreetUser from './components/GreetUser.vue'
export default {
```

```
  components: {
    GreetUser
  }
}
</script>
```

Now, save all your files and open the browser. You should see "Hello Developer" - your first Vue component is up and running!

Before we move on, I want to highlight something. When creating new components, it's common to need a template block, a script block, and possibly a style block to add styling. To help you with this, there's a VS Code extension called "Vue VSCode Snippets" by Sarah Drasner. I highly recommend installing it. This extension provides numerous code snippets to speed up your coding process. Once you have it installed, creating new components becomes incredibly easy.

Let's rewrite the code for the `greet` component using the Vue snippet. Clear all the existing code and type `vbase-css`. You'll see the basic structure for an entire component generated for you. Make the necessary changes: the template will contain an `<h2>` tag with the text "Hello Developer." The default export will have the `name` property. You'll also have a `<style>` block. We'll explore the `scoped` keyword later, but for now, this is where you put the CSS specific to your component. Since we don't have any CSS yet, you can leave it as is. If you format the code, save the file, and refresh the browser, the component should work as expected.

That's the basics of components in Vue. They represent portions of the user interface, are reusable, and can be nested within other components. However, we haven't seen how they are reusable yet. We'll explore that in the next section!

Component Props

Props are like little gifts you give to your components so they can be more versatile and do different things.

Remember how we created our `greet` component in the last section? We could only say "Hello Developer." What if we wanted to greet other people too?

That's where **props** come in. Think of them like custom attributes you add to your components. You can send them values from the parent component (like our main `App` component) and they'll change the component's behavior.

Let's see how it works:

- **Defining Props:** We'll start by adding a `name` prop to our `greet` component. This will let us pass in a name from the `App` component and display it in the greeting.

```
<template>
  <div class="greet">
    <h1>Hello {{ name }}</h1>
  </div>
</template>

<script>
export default {
  props: ['name'], //  We tell the component to expect
a prop named 'name'
  // ... rest of our component
}
</script>
```

- **Passing Props:** Now, in our `App` component, we'll give our `greet` component a `name` attribute with a value.

```
<template>
  <div >
      <GreetUser name="Clark"></GreetUser>
      <GreetUser name="Bruce"></GreetUser>
      <GreetUser name="John"></GreetUser>
  </div>
</template>

<script>
import GreetUser from './components/GreetUser.vue'
export default {
  // ... rest of our App component
      components: {
            GreetUser
      } ,
props: ['name'],
}
</script>
```

- **Using Props in the Template:** In our `greet` component, we can now use the `name` prop inside the template just like a regular data property.

```
<template>
```

```
    <div class="greet">
      <h1>Hello {{ name }}</h1>
    </div>
  </template>
```

Now, if you open your browser, you'll see three greetings: "Hello Bruce", "Hello Clark", and "Hello Diana."

Adding More Props

We can pass multiple props to a component. Let's add another prop called heroName.

```
<template>
  <div class="greet">
    <h1>Hello {{ name }}</h1>
    <p>Also known as {{ heroName }}</p>
  </div>
</template>

<script>
export default {
  props: ['name', 'heroName'],
  // ... rest of our component
}
</script>
```

In our App component:

```
<template>
  <div >
    <GreetUser name="Bruce" heroName="Batman"></GreetUser>
    <GreetUser name="Clark" heroName="Superman"></GreetUser>
    <GreetUser name="Diana" heroName="Wonder
Woman"></GreetUser>
  </div>
</template>
```

Passing Dynamic Values

We can also use dynamic values from our App component's data to set props. Let's say we have a name and a book in our App component's data:

```
<script>
export default {
  data() {
    return {
      name: 'Developer',
      book: "Developer's Guide"
    }
```

```
  } ,
  // ... rest of our App component
}
</script>
```

We can use the v-bind directive to pass these data properties as props:

```
<template>
  <div >
    <GreetUser :name="name" :heroName="book"></GreetUser>
  </div>
</template>
```

Exercise:

Create a new component called profile. It should have two props: name and age. In the template, display the name and age. Create a profile component in your App component and pass in values for name and age.

Solution:

```
// UserProfile.vue
<template>
  <div class="profile">
    <h2>{{ name }}</h2>
    <p>Age: {{ age }}</p>
  </div>
</template>

<script>
export default {
  name: 'UserProfile'
  props: ['name', 'age'],
}
</script>

// App.vue
<template>
  <div >
    <UserProfile name="Jane Doe" age="30"></UserProfile>
  </div>
</template>

<script>
import UserProfile from './components/UserProfile.vue'
export default {
      components: {
                  UserProfile
            } ,
  // ...
```

```
}
</script>
```

Key Takeaways

- Props allow you to pass data from parent components to child components, making your components more reusable.
- Use the `props` array to specify the props a component expects.
- Pass props using attributes in the parent component's template.
- Access props in the child component's template using the mustache syntax.

Prop Types and Validations

In the last section, we learned about component props in Vue. We saw how to pass in both static and dynamic props. In our example, the `App` component was the parent component passing data to the `Greet` component, which was the child component.

Now, we're going to dive deeper into prop types and validations. In our `Greet` component, we had two props: `name` and `heroName`. Without any further information, it's difficult to know what type of data these props expect – a string, an array, an object, or something else.

Vue offers a way to specify the type of each prop, making our code more readable and maintainable. This is especially helpful when working with larger projects or collaborating with other developers.

Let's create a new component called `Article` to illustrate this. In our `components` folder, create a file called `Article.vue`. This component will represent an article in a blog.

```
<template>
  <h2>Article Component</h2>
</template>

<script>
export default {
  props: {
    title: String,
  },
};
</script>
```

We've added a simple `h2` tag displaying "Article Component." The important part is in the `<script>` section where we define the `props` object.

Instead of an array, we're now using an object where the key is the prop name (title) and the value is the prop type (String). We'll bind this prop to our h2 tag, replacing the static text with the dynamic value.

```
<template>
  <h2>{{ title }}</h2>
</template>

<script>
export default {
  props: {
    title: String,
  },
};
</script>
```

Now, in our App component, we'll import and use the Article component, passing in a prop for title.

```
<template>
  <ArticleView title="My First Article" />
</template>

<script>
import ArticleView from './components/ArticleView.vue'
export default {
      components: {
                  ArticleView
            } ,
  // ...
}
</script>
```

If you save and refresh the browser, you'll see "My First Article" displayed!

This approach not only provides documentation but also helps Vue warn us if we pass in the wrong type of data. Let's add another prop to our Article component called likes and set its type to Number.

```
<template>
  <h2>{{ title }}</h2>
  <p>Likes: {{ likes }}</p>
</template>

<script>
export default {
```

```
  props: {
    title: String,
    likes: Number,
  },
};
</script>
```

Now in `App.vue`, we'll pass in the `likes` prop.

```
<template>
  <Article title="My First Article" :likes="50" />
</template>
```

Notice the colon before `likes`. This is the shorthand for `v-bind` which ensures that the value is treated as a number and not a string.

If we forget this and simply pass in `likes="50"`, Vue will warn us in the console:

```
[Vue warn]: Invalid prop type check failed for prop "likes":
expected Number with value 50, got String with value "50".
```

This warning is a great help during development!

Let's also add a boolean prop called `isPublished` to our `Article` component.

```
<template>
  <h2>{{ title }}</h2>
  <p>Likes: {{ likes }}</p>
  <p>Published: {{ isPublished ? 'Yes' : 'No' }}</p>
</template>

<script>
export default {
  props: {
    title: String,
    likes: Number,
    isPublished: Boolean,
  },
};
</script>
```

In `App.vue`, we'll pass in the prop `isPublished` with the value `true`:

```
<template>
  <Article title="My First
Article" :likes="50" :isPublished="true" />
</template>
```

You'll see "Published: Yes" displayed in the browser. Again, if we forget the colon (:) and simply use `isPublished="true"`, we'll get a warning in the console.

Prop Validation: Required Props and Default Values

Besides basic type checks, we can also specify if a prop is required or set a default value.

Let's make the `title` prop mandatory for our `Article` component.

```
<template>
  <h2>{{ title }}</h2>
  <p>Likes: {{ likes }}</p>
  <p>Published: {{ isPublished ? 'Yes' : 'No' }}</p>
</template>

<script>
export default {
  props: {
    title: {
      type: String,
      required: true,
    },
    likes: Number,
    isPublished: Boolean,
  },
};
</script>
```

Now, if we remove the `title` prop from `App.vue`, we'll see a warning in the console:

```
[Vue warn]: Missing required prop: "title".
```

This is very helpful for preventing common errors. We can also set a default value for any prop, including required ones. Let's set a default title for our `Article` component:

```
<template>
  <h2>{{ title }}</h2>
  <p>Likes: {{ likes }}</p>
  <p>Published: {{ isPublished ? 'Yes' : 'No' }}</p>
</template>

<script>
export default {
  props: {
    title: {
      type: String,
      required: true,
```

```
      default: 'Default Article Title',
    },
    likes: Number,
    isPublished: Boolean,
  },
};
</script>
```

Now, if we don't pass in the `title` prop, "Default Article Title" will be displayed. However, if we do provide a `title` prop, that value will be used instead.

Other Prop Types

We've seen examples of string, number, and boolean prop types. Vue also supports other types such as:

- Array
- Object
- Date
- Function

You can explore these on your own!

This concludes our discussion on component props in Vue. We've learned how to define prop types, set required props, and provide default values. This will significantly improve the clarity and maintainability of our Vue applications.

Non-Prop Attributes

Imagine you're creating a component for a blog article. You might pass in things like the title, author, and content as props, right? But what if you want to add an ID to that article element for styling or accessibility? That's where non-prop attributes come in. They're regular HTML attributes like `id`, `class`, or `style` that you can apply directly to your component, even if they don't have corresponding properties in your component's props.

Let's take our blog article example. We have a component called "ArticleView" with a `div` as the root element and a few `h2` headings. In the `App` component, we're calling the `ArticleView` component and passing in props like the `title`, `author`, and `content`.

```
<template>
  <div >
```

```
    <ArticleView :title="'My Blog Article'" :author="'John
Doe'" :content="'This is the content of my article.'" />
    </div>
</template>

<script>
import ArticleView from './ArticleView.vue';

export default {
  components: {
    ArticleView,
  }
}
</script>
```

Now, let's add an `id` attribute to our `ArticleView` component:

```
    <ArticleView id="myArticle" :title="'My Blog Article'" :author="'John
Doe'" :content="'This is the content of my article.'" />
    </div>
```

If we look in the browser's inspector, we'll see the `id="myArticle"` attribute applied directly to the `div` element. That's the default behavior in Vue: when a component returns a single root node, non-prop attributes are automatically added to that root node or the first element where there is no root node.

But what if we don't want to apply the `id` attribute to the root node? What if we want it applied to a specific heading element instead? Vue has a way to do that!

We can use the `v-bind` directive with a special property called `$attrs`. This lets us control which element receives the non-prop attributes.

```
<template>
  <div>
    <h2 v-bind="$attrs">
      {{ title }}
    </h2>
    <h2>{{ author }}</h2>
    <h2>{{ content }}</h2>
  </div>
</template>
```

Now, if we look in the browser, the `id="myArticle"` attribute will be applied to the first `h2` element, which is where we used `v-bind="$attrs"`.

One last thing - sometimes you don't want Vue to automatically apply non-prop attributes to the root node. You can disable this by adding the `inheritAttrs` option to your component and setting it to `false`. It will be applied to the first element after root node instead.

```
<script>
export default {
  props: ['title', 'author', 'content'],
  inheritAttrs: false,
  // ... rest of your component
}
</script>
```

With `inheritAttrs` set to `false`, the non-prop attributes will only be applied to the elements where you explicitly use `v-bind="$attrs"`.

So, that's it for non-prop attributes! You'll see them come up often when you're working with form elements like inputs, selects, and dropdowns. Just remember, you can control how they're applied using `$attrs` and `inheritAttrs`.

Provide and Inject

Imagine a Vue application with a whole bunch of components, starting with the root `App` component. Inside `App`, you have components A, B, and C, each nested with their own children, like D within B and E within C, and F nestled inside E. It's quite a family tree!

Now, say A, D, and F need to display the currently logged-in username. This username is stored in the `App` component. We could pass it down as a prop, but that gets messy with all the nested components.

Passing a prop from `App` to A is easy. But to get it to D, we'd have to pass it to B, and then B to D. The same goes for F, with the prop traveling through C and E.

This "prop-passing-down-the-line" can be a real headache, especially with many levels of components. It's not ideal for things like language preferences, UI themes, or user authentication that multiple components need.

That's where `provide` and `inject` come in! They let us make data accessible across components without the manual prop passing, like a magical data highway for your components.

Let's use our example to see how it works. We'll `provide` the username in the `App` component and `inject` it into `F`. Here's the plan:

- **Provide:** Set the username in the `App` component.
- **Inject:** Grab the username in the `F` component.

Let's head to our code editor and implement these steps.

In the `App` component:

```
<template>
  <div>
    <h3>App Component: {{ name }}</h3>
    <AView />
  </div>
</template>

<script>
import AView from './AView.vue';

export default {
  components: { AView },
  data() {
    return {
      name: 'Developer',
    };
  },
  provide() {
    return {
      username: this.name,
    };
  },
};
</script>
```

Here, we're providing the `username` using `provide()`. We define an object with the property `username` and set its value to `this.name` (which is 'Developer' in this case).

Now, in the `A` component:

```
<template>
  <h3>Component A: {{ username }}</h3>
      <BView />
</template>

<script>
import BView from './BView.vue';

export default {
```

```
  components: { BView },
  inject: ['username'],
};
</script>
```

Now, in the B component:

```
<template>
  <h3>Component B: {{ username }}</h3>
    <CView />
</template>

<script>
import CView from './CView.vue';

export default {
  components: { CView },
  inject: ['username'],
};
</script>
```

Now, in the C component:

```
<template>
  <h3>Component C: {{ username }}</h3>
<DView />
</template>

<script>

import DView from './DView.vue';

export default {
  components: { DView },
  inject: ['username'],
};
</script>
```

Now, in the D component:

```
<template>
  <h3>Component D: {{ username }}</h3>
<FView />
</template>

<script>
import FView from './FView.vue';

export default {
  components: { FView },
  inject: ['username'],
```

```
};
</script>
```

Now, in the `F` **component:**

```
<template>
  <h3>Component F: {{ username }}</h3>
</template>

<script>
export default {
  inject: ['username'],
};
</script>
```

We use the `inject` option, which is an array containing the name of the property we want to inject (`username`).

Now, if you save and open the browser, you should see from "Component A: Developer" to "Component F: Developer" on the screen! We managed to get the username from the `App` component to `F` without passing it through every component in between.

So, there you have it! `provide` and `inject` provide a clean way to share data between components without prop-passing chaos.

Exercise:

Create a new Vue application with a parent component `Parent` and a child component `Child`. In `Parent`, provide a value called `message` with the text "Hello from Parent!". In `Child`, inject `message` and display it on the screen.

Solution:

```
// ParentView.vue
<template>
  <div>
    <Child />
  </div>
</template>

<script>
import Child from './Child.vue';

export default {
  components: { Child },
  provide() {
    return {
```

```
      message: 'Hello from Parent!',
    };
  },
};
</script>

// ChildView.vue
<template>
  <div>
    {{ message }}
  </div>
</template>

<script>
export default {
  inject: ['message'],
};
</script>
```

With this, you'll see "Hello from Parent!" displayed in the `Child` component, demonstrating the power of `provide` and `inject`!

Component Events

Imagine you have a child component, like a pop-up, and you want to send information back to its parent component. That's where custom events come in handy.

Let's create a simple scenario. We'll build an app with a button to open a pop-up. This pop-up will have a "Close" button that hides itself when clicked. We'll use custom events to manage this communication between the parent and child components.

Setting up the Pop-Up Component

First, we'll create a new file in our `components` folder called `PopUp.vue`.

```
<template>
  <div v-show="showPopup">
    <h2>This is a Pop-Up</h2>
    <button @click="$emit('close')">Close Pop-Up</button>
  </div>
</template>

<script>
export default {
  name: 'PopUp',
  props: ['showPopup'],
  emits: ['close'],
};
</script>

<style scoped>
/* Optional styling for your Pop-Up */
</style>
```

In this component, we have a `div` with the `v-show` directive, which will control its visibility. The "Close Pop-Up" button will emit a custom event named "close" when clicked.

Integrating with the Parent Component

Now, we'll update our `App.vue` file to include this `PopUp` component and handle its events.

```
<template>
  <div >
```

```
    <button @click="showPopup = true">Show Pop-up</button>
    <PopUp :showPopup="showPopup" @close="closePopup" />
  </div>
</template>

<script>
import PopUp from './components/PopUp.vue';

export default {
  components: {
    PopUp,
  },
  data() {
    return {
      showPopup: false,
    };
  },
  methods: {
    closePopup() {
      this.showPopup = false;
    },
  },
};
</script>
```

We've imported our `PopUp` component and added it to the `components` object. We're using `v-model` to control the visibility of the pop-up and binding the "close" event from the `PopUp` component to our `closePopup` method in `App.vue`.

Let's break down what's happening:

- `emits` **in** `PopUp.vue`: This array defines the custom events the `PopUp` component can emit. Here, we're emitting the "close" event.
- `$emit('close')` **in** `PopUp.vue`: This line emits the "close" event when the "Close Pop-Up" button is clicked.
- `@close="closePopup"` **in** `App.vue`: This listens for the "close" event emitted by the `PopUp` component and calls the `closePopup` method in the parent component.
- `closePopup` **method in** `App.vue`: This method sets the `showPopup` data property to `false`, effectively hiding the pop-up.

Adding Data Transfer

You can also pass data back to the parent component using custom events. For example, let's say we want to pass the name of the user closing the pop-up.

Update `PopUp.vue`:

```
<template>
  <div>
    <h2>This is a Pop-Up</h2>
    <button @click="$emit('close', 'Developer')">Close Pop-
Up</button>
  </div>
</template>

<script>
export default {
  name: 'PopUp',
  emits: ['close'],
};
</script>

<style scoped>
/* Optional styling for your Pop-Up */
</style>
```

Now, we're passing the string "Developer" as the second argument to `$emit`. We are moving the v-show to parent component, just for you to know another method.

Update `App.vue`:

```
<template>
  <div >
    <button @click="showPopup = true">Show Pop-up</button>
    <PopUp v-show="showPopup" @close="closePopup" />
  </div>
</template>

<script>
import PopUp from './components/PopUp.vue';

export default {
  name: 'App',
  components: {
    PopUp,
  },
  data() {
    return {
      showPopup: false,
    };
  },
```

```
methods: {
    closePopup(name) {
      this.showPopup = false;
      console.log('Name:', name); // Will print "Name:
Developer" to the console
    },
  },
};
</script>
```

The `closePopup` method now takes the data (in this case, the name) as an argument and logs it to the console.

Custom events in Vue provide a robust way to communicate between components. They are fundamental to building complex and modular applications. Now, you can go on to create even more dynamic and interactive applications using custom events in Vue!

Exercise:

Create a simple counter component that displays a count and has buttons to increment and decrement the count. Use custom events to update the count in the parent component.

Solution:

CounterView.vue:

```
<template>
  <div>
    <span>{{ counter }}</span>
    <button @click="$emit('increment')">+</button>
    <button @click="$emit('decrement')">-</button>
  </div>
</template>

<script>
export default {
  name: 'CounterView',
  props: ['counter'],
  emits: ['increment', 'decrement'],
  data() {
    return {
      count: 0,
    };
  },
};
</script>
```

App.vue:

```
<template>
  <div >
    <CounterView :counter="count"
@increment="incrementCount" @decrement="decrementCount" />
  </div>
</template>

<script>
import CounterView from './components/CounterView.vue';

export default {
  name: 'App',
  components: {
    CounterView,
  },
  data() {
    return {
      count: 0,
    };
  },
  methods: {
    incrementCount() {
      this.count++;
    },
    decrementCount() {
      this.count--;
    },
  },
};
</script>
```

This exercise demonstrates how custom events can be used to create interactive components that communicate with their parent components.

Validating Emitted Events

In the previous section, we learned about custom events, which help a child component communicate with its parent component. We use the $emit instance variable to emit an event from the child and handle it in the parent component. Now, just like we can validate props passed into a child component, we can also validate custom events emitted from it. This section will show you how that works with a simple example.

Remember, we have our App component and a Pop-up component nested within it. The App component has a "Show Pop-up" button to display the

Pop-up component, and the Pop-up component has a "Close Pop-up" button that emits an event to the App component. The App component listens to the "close" event and sets its data property to false, which hides the Pop-up component in the browser. Let's quickly see this in action:

```
// App.vue
<template>
  <div>
    <button @click="showPopup = true">Show Pop-up</button>
    <PopUp v-if="showPopup" @close="showPopup =
false"></PopUp>
  </div>
</template>

<script>
import PopUp from './components/PopUp.vue';

export default {
  components: {
    PopUp,
  },
  data() {
    return {
      showPopup: false,
    };
  },
};
</script>

// PopUp.vue
<template>
  <div>
    <button @click="$emit('close')">Close Pop-up</button>
  </div>
</template>

<script>
export default {

};
</script>
```

When you run this code, you'll see a button that, when clicked, displays a pop-up. Clicking the "Close Pop-up" button inside the pop-up will hide the pop-up.

Now, let's improve this by allowing the user to enter a name in the pop-up and sending that name to the parent component when emitting the "close" event.

First, add a new data property to the Pop-up component:

```
// PopUp.vue
<script>
export default {
  data() {
    return {
      name: '',
    };
  },
  // ... rest of the code
};
</script>
```

Next, add an input field to the Pop-up component's template:

```
// PopUp.vue
<template>
  <div>
    <input type="text" v-model="name">
    <button @click="$emit('close', name)">Close Pop-
up</button>
  </div>
</template>
```

You can also wrap the event in a method:

```
// PopUp.vue
<template>
  <div>
    <input type="text" v-model="name">
    <button @click="close">Close Pop-up</button>
  </div>
</template>
<script>
export default {
  // ... rest of the code
  methods: {
    close() {
      this.$emit('close', this.name);
    },
  },
};
</script>
```

Finally, receive user input and log to the console:

```
// App.vue
<template>
```

```
    <div>
      <button @click="showPopup = true">Show Pop-up</button>
      <PopUp v-if="showPopup" @close="closePopup"></PopUp>
    </div>
</template>

<script>
import PopUp from './components/PopUp.vue';

export default {
  components: {
    PopUp,
  },
  data() {
    return {
      showPopup: false,
    };
  },
  methods: {
    closePopup(name) {
      this.showPopup = false;
      console.log('Name:', name); // Will print "Name:
Developer" to the console
    },
  },
};
</script>
```

Now, save the files and refresh the browser. You'll see an input field in the pop-up where you can enter a name. When you click "Close Pop-up," you'll see the name you entered logged in the console of your browser.

Let's add some validation when emitting this event. We start by changing the `emits` option to an object instead of an array. The object contains key-value pairs: the key is the custom event name, and the value is a validation function:

```
// PopUp.vue
<script>
export default {
  // ... rest of the code
  emits: {
    close: (name) => {
      if (!name) {
        return false;
      } else {
        return true;
      }
```

```
    },
  },
};
</script>
```

This validation function receives the argument specified when emitting the event (in our case, `name`). We can add a validation rule within the function's body. Returning `false` will display a warning in the console, while returning `true` means the validation passed. Here, we've added a simple rule: the name cannot be empty.

Now, go back to the browser, open the pop-up, and leave the name input empty. When you click "Close Pop-up," you'll see the warning "Event validation failed for event close" in the console. Now fill in the name input and close the pop-up. You won't see the warning anymore.

This is a simple way to add validations to emitted events. Although these event validations only warn the user in the console, they are incredibly useful when you're working in a team and developing components that will be used by others.

Components and v-model

In this section, we're going to learn how to use the `v-model` directive with a custom component. This might seem a little tricky at first, but it's actually quite simple. Let's dive into the code and see how it works!

We'll start with our `App` component, which has an empty template and an empty data object. Let's add an input element so the user can enter their name:

```
<template>
  <div>
    <input type="text" v-model="name">
  </div>
</template>

<script>
export default {
  data() {
    return {
      name: '',
    };
  },
};
</script>
```

We added a data property called `name` and initialized it to an empty string. Then, we added an input element with `type="text"` and used `v-model="name"` to bind the input element to the `name` data property. Remember, `v-model` is a directive that makes two-way binding possible. It automatically updates the data property when the input changes and vice versa.

Now, if we save and open our browser, we should see our input element. We can type in a name, and that name should be stored in the `name` data property of our `App` component.

Let's verify this using the Vue Devtools. The Vue Devtools is a fantastic tool that allows us to inspect the values of data properties in our components, along with many other things. I highly recommend installing the Vue Devtools for Vue 3. It's really useful for development.

You'll find it in the Chrome Web Store. Once you have it installed, you should see a new tab for Vue in your Chrome Developer Tools. If you click on that tab, you'll see a tree of all the components in your application. Right now, we only have one component, our `App` component. You'll see the data properties listed below, including our `name` property. As you type in the input, you'll see the `name` property update in real-time.

Why are we focusing on the `v-model` directive? Well, often we create custom form components to be used throughout our application. For example, the default HTML input element isn't always styled the way we want it. We might want to create our own input element with custom styles and reuse it in multiple parts of our application. But when we use a custom component, we need to make sure the `v-model` directive works correctly. Let's see how we can do that.

Let's create a new component in our `components` folder called `TextInput.vue`:

```html
<template>
  <input type="text" :value="modelValue">
</template>

<script>
export default {
  props: {
    modelValue: {
      type: String,
      required: true,
    },
  },
};
</script>

<style scoped>
input {
  border: 1px solid #ccc;
  padding: 8px;
  border-radius: 4px;
}
</style>
```

We have a simple input element within our template. We're using `:value="modelValue"` to bind the value of the input to a prop called `modelValue`. We've added a `props` option to define `modelValue` as a required prop of type `String`.

Now, let's import this `TextInput` component into our `App` component and use it instead of the default HTML input:

```
<template>
  <div>
    <TextInput v-model="name" />
    <p> {{ name }} </p>

  </div>
</template>

<script>
import TextInput from './components/TextInput.vue';

export default {
  components: {
    TextInput,
  },
  data() {
    return {
      name: 'default',
    };
  },
};
</script>
```

If we save and refresh our browser, we'll see our custom input element with the custom styling we added in our Input component. You will see 'default' which is the default text we passed. But if we start typing, you'll notice that the name data property in the App component isn't updating. Why is that? It's because the v-model directive doesn't know how to work with our custom component. We need to tell it how to behave.

We need to make a few changes to our Input component:

```
<template>
  <input type="text" :value="modelValue"
@input="$emit('update:modelValue', $event.target.value)">
</template>

<script>
export default {
  props: {
    modelValue: {
      type: String,
      required: true,
    },
  },
  emits: ['update:modelValue'],
};
</script>
```

```
<style scoped>
input {
  border: 1px solid #ccc;
  padding: 8px;
  border-radius: 4px;
}
</style>
```

We've added `@input="$emit('update:modelValue',` `$event.target.value)"` which emits an event called `update:modelValue` whenever the input changes, passing the input value to the parent component.

```
<TextInput v-model="name" />
```

Now, when we use `v-model` with our custom component, it will automatically receive a prop called `modelValue` and listen to the `update:modelValue` event.

```
:value="modelValue"
```

We need to make sure we bind this prop to the `value` attribute of our input element using the `v-bind` directive.

Now, if we save and refresh our browser, we should see our custom input component working as expected. We can type in a name, and the `name` data property will be updated in our `App` component.

So, when building custom form components, remember to handle the `modelValue` prop and `update:modelValue` event to ensure your custom component works with the `v-model` directive. It's a simple process that will allow you to reuse your custom components throughout your application easily.

Exercise

Let's create another custom component, this time a `Select` component, that can be used to select an option from a list. This component should also work with the `v-model` directive.

Solution:

```
<template>
  <select :value="modelValue"
@change="$emit('update:modelValue', $event.target.value)">
    <option v-for="option in
options" :key="option.value" :value="option.value">
      {{ option.label }}
```

```
      </option>
    </select>
</template>

<script>
export default {
  props: {
    modelValue: {
      type: String,
      required: true,
    },
    options: {
      type: Array,
      required: true,
    },
  },
  emits: ['update:modelValue'],
};
</script>
```

This component accepts two props, modelValue and options. The modelValue prop is used to bind the selected value to the parent component, and the options prop is an array of objects containing the label and value of each option.

We're using :value="modelValue" to bind the selected value to the modelValue prop, and @change="$emit('update:modelValue', $event.target.value)" to emit the update:modelValue event with the selected value whenever the selection changes.

We're also using v-for to iterate over the options array and create an option element for each option. We're using :key="option.value" to provide a unique key for each option, and :value="option.value" to set the value of each option.

Now, we can use this Select component in our App component just like we used the Input component. For example:

```
<template>
  <div>
    <SelectComponent v-
model="selectedOption" :options="options" />
    <p> {{ selectedOption }} </p>

  </div>
</template>
```

```
<script>
import SelectComponent from
'./components/SelectComponent.vue';

export default {
  components: {
    SelectComponent,
  },
  data() {
    return {
      selectedOption: '',
      options: [
        { label: 'Option 1', value: 'option1' },
        { label: 'Option 2', value: 'option2' },
        { label: 'Option 3', value: 'option3' },
      ],
    };
  },
};
</script>
```

This will create a select dropdown with the three options defined in the options array. The selectedOption data property will be updated whenever the user selects a different option.

Slots

Remember props? They're awesome for reusing components by passing in different data, but they keep a strict parent-child relationship. The child component always controls the HTML inside, and the parent just sends data.

Slots are more powerful! They also let you reuse components, but the parent component gets to decide what goes inside the child component. It's like a special portal where the parent can send any HTML content right into the child. Let's see how it works!

First, let's create a new component called "CardView." It's a simple card component, like the kind you see on websites to display information. Imagine you want to use this card to show different things, like text, headings, or even images. That's where slots come in.

Create the `CardView`.**vuefile:**

```
<template>
  <div class="card">
    <slot></slot>
  </div>
</template>

<script>
export default {
  name: 'CardView',
};
</script>

<style scoped>
.card {
  border: 1px solid #ccc;
  padding: 10px;
  margin-bottom: 10px;
}
</style>
```

Let's use our Card component in `App.vue`**:**

```
<template>
  <div >
    <CardView>
```

```
      <img src="https://picsum.photos/200/200"
alt="Image" />
        Card Content 1
      </CardView>
      <CardView>
        <img src="https://picsum.photos/200/200"
alt="Image" />
        Card Content 2
      </CardView>
      <CardView>
        <img src="https://picsum.photos/200/200"
alt="Image" />
        Card Content 3
      </CardView>
      <CardView>
        <!-- Nothing between the tags, using the default slot
content -->
      </CardView>
    </div>
</template>

<script>
import CardView from './components/CardView.vue';

export default {
  name: 'App',
  components: {
    CardView,
  },
  setup() {
    return {
    };
  },
};
</script>
```

In our `CardView.vue` component, we can provide default content to be displayed if the parent doesn't specify anything. We add default content inside the `<slot>` tags.

```
<template>
  <div class="card">
    <slot>Default Card Content</slot>
  </div>
</template>
```

You'll see four cards, each with the content specified by the parent component.

Exercise:

Create a new component called `Button`. This component will have a `<button>` element with a `slot` inside. Let the parent component determine the button's text. Add a default text for the button if no content is provided.

Solution:

```
<!-- ButtonView.vue-->
<template>
  <button>
    <slot>Click Me!</slot>
  </button>
</template>

<script>
export default {
  name: 'Button',
};
</script>
```

That's all for now. In the next section, we'll dive into even more advanced ways to use slots, including named slots. Keep practicing!

Named Slots

 Remember in the previous section, we created a card component with a single slot that let us send content from our parent component?

Now, imagine you want to have multiple slots, giving you more control over your component's structure. You can still have a predefined layout in your child component, but the content within those sections can be customized from the parent component. This is super handy for things like layout components, like our card component!

Let's jump into VS Code and see how we can add multiple slots to our card component. We'll start by adding some structure to the CardView.vue file. Our card should have a header, a content area, and a footer. So, we'll add three divs with IDs to represent these sections:

```
<template>
  <div id="card">
    <div id="card-header">
      <slot name="header"></slot>
    </div>
    <div id="card-content">
      <slot></slot>
```

```
    </div>
    <div id="card-footer">
      <slot name="footer"></slot>
    </div>
  </div>
</template>
```

We've added a slot for the header and a slot for the footer. We also kept our original slot for the content.

Why do we need to name our slots? Vue needs to know which slot to put the content in. So, for the header and footer slots, we've used the `name` attribute to give them unique names: "header" and "footer". Notice that the `card-content` slot doesn't have a name - this is the **default slot**. This means it's the one that will be used if a slot is not explicitly named.

Now, let's head over to our `App.vue` component and fill in the content for our newly created slots!

```
<template>
  <div >
    <CardView>
      <template v-slot:header>
        <h3>Header</h3>
      </template>
      <template v-slot:default>
        <img src="https://images.unsplash.com/photo-
1551434686-fa0725284ca6?ixlib=rb-
4.0.3&ixid=MnwxMjA3fDB8MHxwaG90by1wYWdlfHx8fGVufDB8fHx8&auto
=format&fit=crop&w=687&q=80" alt="Image">
      </template>
      <template v-slot:footer>
        <button>View Details</button>
      </template>
    </CardView>
  </div>
</template>
```

Inside our `Card` component, we're using the `v-slot` directive to tell Vue where to place the content. You'll notice that we use a `template` tag for each slot, and then we specify the slot name after the colon in `v-slot`. For example, we have `v-slot:header`, `v-slot:default`, and `v-slot:footer`.

We're placing an `h3` with "Header" inside the `header` slot, an image inside the `default` slot, and a button inside the `footer` slot. Save the file and check your browser - you'll see our card component now has a header, content, and footer, just like we intended!

Remember, this example is just a basic demonstration. In a real-world app, you could use this approach to create more complex components like modals. You could have a modal header, modal content, and a modal footer, and control the content within each section by using named slots.

Slots Props

Let's talk about **slot props**. This is a cool feature that lets you control how your components display information. Think of it like this: imagine you have a reusable component like a name list, but you want different parts of your app to display that name list in different ways. Slot props give you that flexibility.

Let's build a simple example to see how it works. First, we'll create a new component called `NameList.vue` in our `components` folder. We'll use a little CSS trick to make it look nice, but don't worry too much about that right now.

```
<template>
  <div>
    <h3>
      <template v-for="name in
names" :key="name.lastName">
        <slot v-bind="name">
          <p>{{ name.firstName }} {{ name.lastName }}</p>
        </slot>
      </template>
    </h3>
  </div>
</template>

<script>
export default {
  data() {
    return {
      names: [
        { firstName: 'Bruce', lastName: 'Wayne' },
        { firstName: 'Clark', lastName: 'Kent' },
        { firstName: 'Princess', lastName: 'Diana' },
      ],
    };
  },
};
</script>
```

```
<style scoped>
.h3 {
  font-size: 24px;
}
</style>
```

This component has a simple h3 tag with a slot inside. That slot is where the parent component will add its own content.

Now, let's use this NameList component in our App.vue file. We'll import it, add it to our components list, and then use it in our template:

```
<template>
  <div >
    <NameList />
  </div>
</template>

<script>
import NameList from './components/NameList.vue';

export default {
  components: {
    NameList,
  },
};
</script>
```

If you run this code, you'll see the list of names being displayed. But what if we want to customize how those names are shown? That's where slot props come in!

Let's go back to our NameList.vue component and add some slot props:

```
<template>
  <div>
    <h3>
      <template v-for="name in names" :key="name.lastName">
      <p>
      <slot :first-name="name.firstName" :last-
name="name.lastName"></slot>
      </p>
      </template>

    </h3>
  </div>
</template>

<script>
```

```
export default {
  data() {
    return {
      names: [
        { firstName: 'Bruce', lastName: 'Wayne' },
        { firstName: 'Clark', lastName: 'Kent' },
        { firstName: 'Princess', lastName: 'Diana' },
      ],
    };
  },
};
</script>
```

We've added two props to the slot: first-name and last-name. We're using the v-bind directive shorthand (:), and we're passing the firstName and lastName values from our name object to the parent component.

Now, in our App.vue file, we can use those slot props to control how the names are displayed:

```
<template>
  <div >
    <NameList>
      <template v-slot:default="{ firstName, lastName }">
        {{ firstName }} {{ lastName }}
      </template>
    </NameList>

    <NameList>
      <template v-slot:default="{ firstName, lastName }">
        {{ lastName }}, {{ firstName }}
      </template>
    </NameList>

    <NameList>
      <template v-slot:default="{ firstName, lastName }">
        {{ firstName }}
      </template>
    </NameList>
  </div>
</template>

<script>
import NameList from './components/NameList.vue';

export default {
  components: {
    NameList,
```

```
   },
};
</script>
```

We're using the `v-slot` directive to tell Vue that this template belongs to the `slot` in the `NameList` component. We're also using the curly braces `{}` to get the values of the slot props (`firstName` and `lastName`) that were sent from the child component. The 'default' indicate that the slot is the default slot, not a named slot.

Sample:

```
<NameList>
    <template v-slot:slotName="{ firstName, lastName }">
       {{ firstName }} {{ lastName }}
    </template>
</NameList>
```

If you named a slot, you will pass the name instead.

Now, you can see how the `NameList` component is displaying the names differently in each instance because of the slot props.

Let's Recap!

- **Slot props** let you pass data from a child component to the parent component, specifically within a slot.
- You use the `v-bind` directive shorthand (`:`) on the `slot` in the child component to pass the data.
- In the parent component, use the `v-slot` directive to access the slot props and use them in your template.

Exercise:

Create a new component called `ProductCard.vue` that displays information about a product. Use slot props to pass the product name, price, and image to the parent component. Let the parent component control how the product information is displayed.

Solution:

```
<!-- ProductCard.vue -->
<template>
  <div>
    <slot v-bind="product" ></slot>
  </div>
</template>
```

```
<script>
export default {
  data() {
    return {
      product: {
        name: 'Awesome Gadget',
        price: 19.99,
        image: 'https://example.com/product-image.jpg',
      },
    };
  },
};
</script>

<!-- App.vue -->
<template>
  <div >
    <ProductCard>
      <template v-slot:default="{ name, price, image }">
        <h2>{{ name }}</h2>
        <p>Price: ${{ price }}</p>
        <img :src="image" alt="{{ name }}" />
      </template>
    </ProductCard>
  </div>
</template>

<script>
import ProductCard from './components/ProductCard.vue';

export default {
  components: {
    ProductCard,
  },
};
</script>
```

So, that's it! Now you have a solid understanding of slot props and how they can make your components even more flexible and reusable.

Component Styles

In this section, we're diving into a fundamental concept when working with component in Vue: **global versus scoped styling**.

We'll explore three key points, each with a clear example. But first, let's set up our components.

We'll start by creating a new file in the `components` folder called `ChildStyles.vue`. We'll use the `vbase-css` snippet to quickly create a Vue component, naming it "ChildStyles.vue". Notice the `scoped` attribute on the `style` block - we'll cover that soon!

```
<template>
  <div>
    <h4>Child Styles Component</h4>
  </div>
</template>

<script>
export default {
  name: 'ChildStyles'
};
</script>

<style>
</style>
```

Next, let's add this component to our `App.vue` file:

```
<template>
  <h4>App Component</h4>
  <ChildStyles />
</template>

<script>
import ChildStyles from './components/ChildStyles.vue';

export default {
  components: {
    ChildStyles
  }
};
</script>

<style>
</style>
```

Now, let's jump into our first point: **Global Styles**. In the `App.vue` component's `style` block, let's add a style rule to change the color of all `h4` elements to orange:

```
<style>
h4 {
  color: orange;
}
</style>
```

If we save the file and check the browser, you'll see both the "App Component" and "Child Styles Component" text is orange!

You might be thinking, "Well, the parent component's styles are being applied to the child component, right?" You're absolutely right!

But it's not just that. Let's move that `h4` style rule from the `App.vue` component into the `ChildStyles.vue` component, changing the color to olive for better clarity:

```
<style scoped>
h4 {
  color: olive;
}
</style>
```

Now, you'll notice that **both** the "App Component" and "Child Styles Component" text is olive!

This is our first key point: By default, a component's styles are applied **globally** throughout the component tree. This means that even though you've defined styles within a specific component, they can affect elements in other components. Regular CSS rules also apply here, so if you have two `h4` elements, one with a style of olive and the other with a style of orange, the parent's style (orange) will be applied because the parent's style is evaluated last.

So, how do we style the `h4` tag in the `ChildStyles.vue` component so that it only affects the `ChildStyles.vue` component? This brings us to our second point: **Scoped Styles**.

To make sure a component's styles only apply to its own template, we need to add the `scoped` attribute to the `style` tag. Let's add it to the `App.vue` component:

```
<style scoped>
h4 {
```

```
    color: orange;
}
</style>
```

Now, save the file and take a look at the browser. You'll see that the orange color is now only applied to the "App Component" text, and the "Child Styles Component" text is still olive.

Let's add the `scoped` attribute to the `ChildStyles.vue` component as well:

```
<style scoped>
h4 {
    color: olive;
}
</style>
```

We've now successfully isolated the olive styling to the `ChildStyles.vue` component!

Our second point: The `scoped` attribute ensures a component's CSS only applies to its own HTML elements.

But here's a catch! This isn't always completely true. There's a special case: **the root node**. If you remove the wrapping `div` tag in `ChildStyles.vue`, you'll find that even with the `scoped` attribute, the "App Component" text still turns olive. The "App Component" text is now considered the root node of the `ChildStyles.vue` component!

The documentation states that "the parent component's styles will not leak into child components, however a child component's root node will be affected by both the parent's scoped CSS and the child's scoped CSS." This is designed to allow the parent component to style the child's root node for layout purposes.

To avoid this behavior, you can use CSS Modules, but that's a topic for another time.

Scoped Styles with Slots.

Add the wrapping `div` tag and `scoped` attribute back to the `ChildStyles.vue` component to ensure we have our orange and olive text. Now, instead of directly adding an `h4` tag within the `ChildStyles.vue` component, we'll use a `slot`. Let's also convert `ChildStyles` into opening and closing tags within the `App.vue` component and add the `h4` element between the tags:

```
<!-- ChildStyles.vue -->
<template>
  <div>
    <slot />
  </div>
</template>

<style scoped>
h4 {
  color: olive;
}
</style>

<!-- App.vue -->
<template>
  <h4>App Component</h4>
  <ChildStyles>
    <h4>Child Styles Component</h4>
  </ChildStyles>
</template>
```

If we save and refresh, you'll see both elements are now orange!

Our third point: When using slots, the parent component's styles are applied, not the child component's styles, even though the content is embedded within the child component. This is because the slot itself is treated as an element of the parent component.

So there you have it! Now you understand the nuances of component styling in Vue. Global versus scoped styles, the impact of the `scoped` attribute, and the behavior of slots!

Dynamic Components

Let's dive into dynamic components in Vue. This is a powerful feature that makes your code more manageable and efficient, especially when working with many components.

Imagine you're building a website with tabs. You have three tabs, "Tab A," "Tab B," and "Tab C," and each tab displays different content. Clicking on a tab should display the corresponding content while hiding the others.

Building the Basics

First, we need to create our basic components. In your project's components folder, create three new files: TabA.vue, TabB.vue, and TabC.vue. These will be our individual tab components.

Inside TabA.vue, add the following:

```
<template>
  <div>
    <h1>Tab A Content</h1>
  </div>
</template>

<script>
export default {
  name: 'TabA',
};
</script>

<style scoped>

</style>
```

Copy and paste this code into TabB.vue and TabC.vue, updating the <h1> content to "Tab B Content" and "Tab C Content," respectively.

Adding the Tabbed Interface

Now, let's add the tabbed interface to our main App.vue component:

```
<template>
  <div>
    <button @click="activeTab = 'TabA'">Tab A</button>
    <button @click="activeTab = 'TabB'">Tab B</button>
    <button @click="activeTab = 'TabC'">Tab C</button>
```

```
    <component :is="activeTab"></component>
  </div>
</template>

<script>
import TabA from './components/TabA.vue';
import TabB from './components/TabB.vue';
import TabC from './components/TabC.vue';

export default {
  name: 'App',
  components: {
    TabA,
    TabB,
    TabC,
  },
  data() {
    return {
      activeTab: 'TabA',
    };
  },
};
</script>
```

Now, run your application! You'll see the basic tabs interface. Clicking on a tab will change the displayed content.

Why Use Dynamic Components?

- **Maintainability:** Instead of listing all your components within the template and using `v-if` directives, dynamic components offer a cleaner approach.
- **Flexibility:** Dynamic components make it easier to switch between components without rewriting a bunch of code. Imagine having a multi-step form with 80 steps! Dynamic components make it manageable.
- **Efficiency:** Vue only renders the currently active component. This improves performance, especially in complex applications.

Exercise:

Create a new component called `TabD.vue`. Add it to your `components` object in `App.vue`. Create a new tab button to activate `TabD` and add some content to `TabD.vue`.

Solution:

Add `TabD.vue` to your `components` folder:

```
<template>
  <div>
    <h1>Tab D Content</h1>
  </div>
</template>

<script>
export default {
  name: 'TabD',
};
</script>

<style scoped>

</style>
```

Then, in `App.vue`, add `TabD` to the `components` object:

```
<script>
import TabA from './components/TabA.vue';
import TabB from './components/TabB.vue';
import TabC from './components/TabC.vue';
import TabD from './components/TabD.vue';

export default {
  // ... other code
  components: {
    TabA,
    TabB,
    TabC,
    TabD,
  },
  // ... other code
};
</script>
```

Finally, add the tab button in your template:

```
<template>
  <div>
    <button @click="activeTab = 'TabA'">Tab A</button>
    <button @click="activeTab = 'TabB'">Tab B</button>
    <button @click="activeTab = 'TabC'">Tab C</button>
    <button @click="activeTab = 'TabD'">Tab D</button>

    <component :is="activeTab"></component>
  </div>
</template>
```

Run your application to see `Tab D` in action!

Keeping Dynamic Components Alive

In the previous section, we learned about dynamic components. We used the `<component>` HTML tag with the `is` attribute, which pointed to a component name that Vue should render in the browser. In this section, we'll explore another feature of dynamic components.

To understand this new feature, let's look at an example. Imagine a user filling out a multi-step form. Each tab represents a different form for the user to enter details. Let's say the user needs to enter their name in the "Tab C" component. We'll add a data property called `name`, initialized to an empty string, and in the template, we'll add an input element for the user to enter their name.

```
<template>
  <div>
    <input type="text" v-model="name">
  </div>
</template>

<script>
export default {
  data() {
    return {
      name: '',
    };
  },
};
</script>
```

We sync this input with the `name` property using the `v-model` directive. If we save the file and head to the browser, we should see the input element in the "Tab C" content. We can type in our name, "Developer," for example.

However, if we switch to "Tab A" and then back to "Tab C," the name we entered will disappear. This happens because each time you switch to a new tab, Vue creates a new instance of the active tab component. In our example, "Tab C" would be recreated.

While this is generally the desired behavior, sometimes we want to cache the component instance once it's created. In our example, it makes sense to preserve the form state when the user switches between tabs and avoid recreating the instance. This is where the `keep-alive` element comes in.

The `keep-alive` element is another custom HTML element specific to Vue. Back in our code editor, we simply wrap the `<component>` tag with the `<keep-alive>` tag:

```
<template>
  <keep-alive>
    <component :is="activeTab"></component>
  </keep-alive>
</template>
```

Now, if we go back to the browser, navigate to "Tab C" content, fill in the name "Developer," click on "Tab A," and switch back to "Tab C," the name "Developer" will still be there. Vue is keeping the dynamic component alive, even though it's inactive.

The `keep-alive` tag is recommended when you need to maintain the state of a dynamic component, even when it's inactive, or if you want to prevent the component from re-rendering for performance reasons.

Teleport Component

"Teleporting? In a web app?" But this new feature is pretty cool, and it's super useful for situations where you want to move a component to a completely different location in your web page.

Imagine you want to display a pop-up window. This pop-up window should be placed above everything else, right? Normally, you'd have to figure out how to move it around in your HTML structure. But, with Vue 3's teleport component, you can easily place it directly within a specific section of your page.

Getting Started with Teleport

First, let's understand where our components normally live. We've got an HTML file, `index.html`, which has a special `div` tag with the ID "app". This `div` is like our main entrance to the Vue.js. All the components we build within Vue.js are placed within this `div`.

```
<!DOCTYPE html>
<html lang="en">
<head>
    <meta charset="UTF-8">
    <meta name="viewport" content="width=device-width,
initial-scale=1.0">
    <title>Vue.js App</title>
</head>
<body>
    <div ></div>

</body>
</html>
```

Now, the teleport component lets us break out of this "app" structure and place a component somewhere else in our HTML. Here's how we do it:

- **Create a New Target:** We need a place to teleport our component to. So, let's add another `div` tag in our `index.html` file, right after the `app` div.

```
<div ></div>
<div id="portal-root"></div>
```

We'll name this div "portal-root".

Make a Component: Let's create a simple component called "Portal" to teleport. Go to your `components` folder and create a new file called `portal.vue`.

```
<template>
  <h2>Portal Component</h2>
</template>
```

And then import it into our main app component:

```
<template>
  <div>
    <portal />
  </div>
</template>
```

Teleportation Time: Now, wrap our `portal` component with the `teleport` component.

```
<template>
  <div>
    <teleport to="#portal-root">
      <portal />
    </teleport>
  </div>
</template>
```

The `teleport` component takes an attribute called "to". Inside this attribute, we put a CSS selector that points to the element we want to teleport to. In this case, it's our "portal-root" `div`.

Take a look at the browser! You should now see the "Portal Component" text inside the "portal-root" section of your page.

Why Teleport?

Now, why would we want to do all this teleportation? Here's a common scenario:

Imagine you're creating a pop-up window. You might want it to be placed right on top of the page, separate from the rest of your application. This is where the teleport component shines.

Let's imagine you have a simple modal pop-up.

```
<template>
  <div class="container">
    <div class="content">
      <button @click="showModal = true">Show Modal</button>
```

```
        <teleport to="#portal-root">
          <div v-if="showModal" class="modal">
            <div class="modal-content">
              <slot />
              <button @click="showModal =
false">Close</button>
            </div>
          </div>
        </teleport>
      </div>
    </div>
</template>
<script>
export default {
  data() {
    return {
      showModal: false,
    };
  },
};
</script>
<style scoped>
.container {
  display: flex;
  justify-content: center;
  align-items: center;
  height: 100vh;
}
.content {
  max-width: 400px;
  position: relative;
}
.modal {
  position: fixed;
  top: 0;
  left: 0;
  width: 100%;
  height: 100%;
  background-color: rgba(0, 0, 0, 0.5);
  display: flex;
  justify-content: center;
  align-items: center;
}
.modal-content {
  background-color: white;
  padding: 20px;
  border-radius: 5px;
}
```

```
</style>
```

Without teleporting, the modal would be restricted by the parent container, and the background wouldn't cover the entire page. With teleport, it's placed directly in the `#portal-root` element, allowing it to display correctly.

You might be wondering why we don't just use HTML elements like `div` and `span` for moving things around. Here's why the `teleport` component is so special:

- **Structure Stays Clean:** Using `teleport` keeps the logical structure of your Vue components intact. Even though your modal is moved, it still acts like a child component of its parent.
- **Event Handling:** Events like clicks or mouseovers that happen within your teleported component will still work correctly, even though the component is not in the original HTML structure.

And that's it for the teleport component! This is just the tip of the iceberg for Vue.js 3. There's so much more to learn! So, keep exploring!

HTTP and Vue

Now, we're going to dive into a super important topic: how Vue works with HTTP requests. Think of it like this - Vue is amazing at building user interfaces, but it doesn't actually know how to talk to servers. It needs a little help to fetch information or send data back and forth.

So, how do we make those connections happen? Well, that's where HTTP libraries come in. They act like translators, allowing Vue to understand and communicate with servers. There are a few popular ones out there, like Axios and fetch API, but for this section, we're going to use Axios. It's a powerful and easy-to-use library, perfect for beginners.

Imagine a website showing you the latest news articles. The articles wouldn't magically appear on the page! They're actually fetched from a server using HTTP requests. Vue doesn't know how to do that directly, so we use Axios to get the data and then display it on the webpage.

Let's get started by adding Axios to our Vue project!

Open your terminal within your project folder and run the command:

```
npm install axios
```

This will download Axios and install it as a dependency for your project.

Now, you'll see Axios listed in your project's `package.json` file. This means it's ready to use.

Fetching Data with GET Requests

We'll learn how to make a GET request to a JSON Placeholder API and display the retrieved data in our web application.

Imagine you're building a blog application. You need to fetch posts from a remote server, display them on your website, and allow users to interact with them. This is exactly where making HTTP requests come into play.

We'll be using a free online REST API called **JSON Placeholder** to practice making these requests. It's perfect for testing and prototyping because it provides a wide variety of fake data without needing to create an actual backend API.

First, let's create a new Vue component to handle our post data. In your
`components` folder, create a new file named `PostList.vue`. Inside the file,
use the `vbase` snippet to quickly generate a basic component structure.

```
<template>
  <div>
    <!-- Content here -->
  </div>
</template>

<script>
export default {
  name: 'PostList',
  data() {
    return {
      // Data properties will go here
    }
  },
  methods: {
    // Methods will go here
  }
}
</script>

<style scoped>
/* Styles here */
</style>
```

Now, let's import this component into our `App.vue` file:

```
<template>
  <div>
    <PostList />
  </div>
</template>

<script>
import PostList from './components/PostList.vue';

export default {
  components: {
    PostList
  }
}
</script>
```

With this, our `PostList` component will be rendered on the webpage.
Let's add a button to trigger our data fetching process.

```
<template>
```

```
<div>
  <button @click="getPosts">Load Posts</button>
</div>
</template>
```

This button will call the `getPosts` method, which we'll define in a moment.

Fetching Data with Axios

To make HTTP requests in Vue.js, we'll use a library called **Axios**.

1. Importing Axios: First, let's import Axios into our `PostList.vue` component:

```
<script>
import axios from 'axios';
// Rest of the component code
</script>
```

2. Creating a Data Property: Next, let's create a data property to store our fetched posts:

```
<script>
export default {
  // ...
  data() {
    return {
      posts: []
    }
  },
  // ...
}
</script>
```

We'll initialize it as an empty array, which will be filled with data later.

3. Defining the `getPosts` **Method:** Now, let's define the `getPosts` method, which will handle our GET request:

```
<script>
export default {
  // ...
  methods: {
    getPosts() {

axios.get('https://jsonplaceholder.typicode.com/posts')
      .then(response => {
        this.posts = response.data;
      })
```

```
      .catch(error => {
        console.error('Error retrieving data:', error);
      });
    }
  }
  // ...
}
</script>
```

This method does the following:

- It uses the `axios.get()` method to send a GET request to the JSON Placeholder API endpoint `/posts`.
- It utilizes the `then()` block to handle the successful response. Inside this block, we assign the retrieved data to our `posts` data property.
- It uses the `catch()` block to handle any potential errors during the request. We log the error to the console for debugging purposes.

4. Rendering the Data: Finally, let's display the fetched posts in our template. We'll use the `v-for` directive to iterate over the `posts` array and render each post's details:

```
<template>
  <div>
    <button @click="getPosts">Load Posts</button>
    <ul>
      <li v-for="post in posts" :key="post.id">
        <h3>{{ post.title }}</h3>
        <p>{{ post.body }}</p>
      </li>
    </ul>
  </div>
</template>
```

This code renders an unordered list (`<ul>`) where each post is displayed as a list item (`<li>`). We use the `:key` attribute to provide a unique identifier for each list item, which helps Vue optimize rendering.

```
<template>
  <div>
    <button @click="getPosts">Load Posts</button>
    <ul>
      <li v-for="post in posts" :key="post.id">
        <h3>{{ post.title }}</h3>
        <p>{{ post.body }}</p>
      </li>
    </ul>
  </div>
</template>
```

```
<script>
import axios from 'axios';
export default {
  name: 'PostList',
  data() {
    return {
      // Data properties will go here
      posts: []
    }
  },
  methods: {
    getPosts() {

axios.get('https://jsonplaceholder.typicode.com/posts')
        .then(response => {
          this.posts = response.data;
        })
        .catch(error => {
          console.error('Error retrieving data:', error);
        });
    }
  },
}
</script>

<style scoped>
/* Styles here */
</style>
```

Now, save all your changes and open your browser. You should see the Load Posts button. Clicking this button will trigger the getPosts method, fetch data from the API, and then display the retrieved posts in the list.

Handling Errors

It's important to provide a user-friendly way to handle potential errors during data fetching. We can add an error message in the template if the API request fails:

```
<template>
  <div>
    <button @click="getPosts">Load Posts</button>
    <p v-if="errorMessage">Error: {{ errorMessage }}</p>
    <ul>
```

```
        <li v-for="post in posts" :key="post.id">
          <h3>{{ post.title }}</h3>
          <p>{{ post.body }}</p>
        </li>
      </ul>
    </div>
</template>

<script>
import axios from 'axios';
export default {
  name: 'PostList',
  data() {
    return {
      // Data properties will go here
      posts: [],
  errorMessage: ''
    }
  },
  methods: {
    getPosts() {
      axios.get('https://jsonplaceholder.typicode.com/posts')
        .then(response => {
          this.posts = response.data;
          this.errorMessage = ''; // Clear error message on
success
        })
        .catch(error => {
          console.error('Error retrieving data:', error);
          this.errorMessage = 'Error retrieving data';
        });
    }
  },
}
</script>

<style scoped>
/* Styles here */
</style>
```

We added an `errorMessage` data property to store the error message. If there's an error, we set `errorMessage` to a relevant message, which is then displayed in the template using `v-if`.

Exercise:

Modify the code to also fetch the user associated with each post.

Hint: The JSON Placeholder API has an endpoint for users at /users. You can access the user ID for each post in post.userId.

Solution:

```
<script>
export default {
  // ...
  data() {
    return {
      posts: [],
      users: [],
      errorMessage: ''
    }
  },
  methods: {
    getPosts() {

axios.get('https://jsonplaceholder.typicode.com/posts')
        .then(response => {
          this.posts = response.data;
          // Fetch users in parallel
          response.data.forEach(post => {
            if (!this.users[post.userId]) {

axios.get(`https://jsonplaceholder.typicode.com/users/$
{post.userId}`)
                .then(userResponse => {
                  this.users[post.userId] =
userResponse.data;
                })
                .catch(error => {
                  console.error('Error fetching user:',
error);
                });
            }
          });
        })
        .catch(error => {
          console.error('Error retrieving data:', error);
          this.errorMessage = 'Error retrieving data';
        });
    }
  }
}
</script>

<template>
  <div>
```

```
   <button @click="getPosts">Load Posts</button>
   <p v-if="errorMessage">Error: {{ errorMessage }}</p>
   <ul>
     <li v-for="post in posts" :key="post.id">
       <h3>{{ post.title }}</h3>
       <p>{{ post.body }}</p>
       <p>Author: {{ users[post.userId]?.name }}</p>
     </li>
   </ul>
 </div>
</template>
```

In the solution, we fetch each user in parallel using the `forEach` loop. This will improve the performance as we're not waiting for one user to be fetched before fetching the next.

We also used the optional chaining operator `?.` to avoid errors if a user is not found in the `users` object.

POST Request

Remember that when we want to create a new resource on an API, we use the HTTP POST request method. To illustrate this, we'll create a simple component that lets you input data for a new post and submit it to the API.

Let's Get Started

First, create a new Vue component file named "CreatePost.vue" inside your `components` folder.

```
<template>
  <div>
    <h1>Create a New Post</h1>
    <form @submit.prevent="createPost">
      <div>
        <label for="userId">Post User ID:</label>
        <input type="text" id="userId" v-
model="formData.userId">
      </div>
      <div>
        <label for="title">Title:</label>
        <input type="text" id="title" v-
model="formData.title">
      </div>
      <div>
        <label for="body">Body:</label>
        <textarea id="body"
```

```
v-model="formData.body"></textarea>
      </div>
      <button type="submit">Create Post</button>
    </form>
  </div>
</template>

<script>
import axios from 'axios';

export default {
  data() {
    return {
      formData: {
        userId: '',
        title: '',
        body: ''
      }
    };
  },
  methods: {
    createPost() {

axios.post('https://jsonplaceholder.typicode.com/posts',
this.formData)
        .then(response => {
          console.log('Response:', response);
        })
        .catch(error => {
          console.error('Error:', error);
        });
    }
  }
};
</script>

<style scoped>
/* Add any styles here if you need them */
</style>
```

Make sure to import the CreatePost component into your main app component and add it to the template:

```
// App.vue

<template>
  <div >
    <CreatePost />
  </div>
```

```
</template>

<script>
import CreatePost from './components/CreatePost.vue';

export default {
  components: {
    CreatePost
  }
};
</script>
```

Now, launch your Vue app and test it out! Enter some values into the input fields and click "Create Post". You should see the response, containing the newly created post data, displayed in your browser's console.

Exercise

Try modifying the CreatePost component to include a simple success message after the post is successfully created. You could even use the newly received post data to display some information on the screen.

Solution

```
<template>
  <div>
    <h1>Create a New Post</h1>
    <form @submit.prevent="createPost">
      <div>
        <label for="userId">Post User ID:</label>
        <input type="text" id="userId" v-
model="formData.userId">
      </div>
      <div>
        <label for="title">Title:</label>
        <input type="text" id="title" v-
model="formData.title">
      </div>
      <div>
        <label for="body">Body:</label>
        <textarea id="body"
v-model="formData.body"></textarea>
      </div>
      <button type="submit">Create Post</button>
    </form>
    <p v-if="postCreated">Post created successfully!</p>
  </div>
</template>
```

```
<script>
import axios from 'axios';

export default {
  data() {
    return {
      formData: {
        userId: '',
        title: '',
        body: ''
      },
    postCreated: false
    };
  },
  methods: {
    createPost() {

axios.post('https://jsonplaceholder.typicode.com/posts',
this.formData)
        .then(response => {
          console.log('Response:', response);
            this.postCreated = true; // Set flag to display
success message
        })
        .catch(error => {
          console.error('Error:', error);
        });
    }
  }
};
</script>

<style scoped>
/* Add any styles here if you need them */
</style>
```

With this simple setup, you've learned how to make POST requests in Vue.js using Axios. You can apply this knowledge to build more complex interactions with APIs and dynamically update your Vue applications.

Lifecycle Hooks

Think of it like the life cycle of a butterfly, where a component goes through different stages in its journey within a Vue application. We have four primary phases: creation, mounting, updating, and unmounting.

Lifecycle hooks are special methods that let us tap into these phases and execute code at specific moments. There are 13 hooks in total, but we'll focus on the ones you're most likely to use. Let's break down each phase and its associated hooks:

Creation Phase: This is where your component is born!

- `beforeCreate`: This hook is called before the component's data properties, computed properties, methods, and watchers are processed. It's not very common to use it in practice.
- `created`: This is your go-to hook for the creation phase. It's called after the component's properties are set up. This is the perfect place to make API calls to fetch data, initialize variables, or set up initial state.

Let's see an example:

```
// Example Component:
export default {
  data() {
    return {
      message: '',
    };
  },
  created() {
    console.log('Component created!');
    // Fetch data from an API
    fetch('https://api.example.com/data')
      .then((response) => response.json())
      .then((data) => {
        this.message = data.message;
      });
  },
};
```

Mounting Phase: This is when the component's template gets attached to the DOM (Document Object Model) and becomes visible on your webpage.

- `beforeMount`: This hook is called right before the component is rendered. It's useful for making DOM manipulations that need to happen before the initial render.

- `mounted`: This is the most commonly used hook in this phase. It's called after the component is rendered and the DOM is ready for access. You can use this hook to access elements in the DOM, attach event listeners, or perform any DOM-related tasks.

Updating Phase: This phase gets triggered whenever a reactive property like your data or computed properties changes, causing the component to re-render.

- `beforeUpdate`: This hook is called before the DOM is updated, giving you a chance to access the old DOM before it gets changed. You might use this to remove event listeners that are no longer needed after the update.
- `updated`: This hook is called after the DOM is updated. Similar to `mounted`, you can perform DOM-dependent operations here.

Unmounting Phase: This is the final phase where your component is removed from the DOM.

- `beforeUnmount`: This hook is called before the component is unmounted. It's a good place to clean up resources like cancelling network requests, removing event listeners, or clearing timers.
- `unmounted`: This hook is called after the component is unmounted. You're unlikely to use this hook often, as the component is already removed from the DOM at this point.

Miscellaneous Methods:

- `activated` & `deactivated`: These hooks are related to the `keep-alive` component. `activated` is called when a component is re-activated after being cached, while `deactivated` is called when it is deactivated.
- `errorCaptured`: This hook is called when an error occurs in any descendant component. You can use it to display an error message or handle the error in a more controlled way.
- `renderTracked` & `renderTriggered`: These hooks are useful for debugging purposes, helping you understand why your component is re-rendering.

Order of Execution

To get a better understanding of how these hooks are called, let's look at an example:

Parent Component (parent.vue):

```html
<template>
  <div>
    Parent Component
    <button @click="toggleChild">Toggle Child</button>
    <div v-if="showChild">
      <child-component />
    </div>
  </div>
</template>

<script>
import ChildComponent from
'./components/ChildComponent.vue';

export default {
  components: {
    ChildComponent,
  },
  data() {
    return {
      showChild: true,
    };
  },
  methods: {
    toggleChild() {
      this.showChild = !this.showChild;
    },
  },
  // Lifecycle Hooks for Parent Component
  beforeCreate() { console.log('Parent Component:
beforeCreate'); },
  created() { console.log('Parent Component: created'); },
  beforeMount() { console.log('Parent Component:
beforeMount'); },
  mounted() { console.log('Parent Component: mounted'); },
  beforeUpdate() { console.log('Parent Component:
beforeUpdate'); },
  updated() { console.log('Parent Component: updated'); },
  beforeUnmount() { console.log('Parent Component:
beforeUnmount'); },
  unmounted() { console.log('Parent Component:
unmounted'); },
};
</script>
```

Child Component (ChildComponent.vue):

```html
<template>
```

```
  <div>Child Component</div>
</template>

<script>
export default {
  // Lifecycle Hooks for Child Component
  beforeCreate() { console.log('Child Component:
beforeCreate'); },
  created() { console.log('Child Component: created'); },
  beforeMount() { console.log('Child Component:
beforeMount'); },
  mounted() { console.log('Child Component: mounted'); },
  beforeUpdate() { console.log('Child Component:
beforeUpdate'); },
  updated() { console.log('Child Component: updated'); },
  beforeUnmount() { console.log('Child Component:
beforeUnmount'); },
  unmounted() { console.log('Child Component:
unmounted'); },
};
</script>
```

- **On Page Load:**
```
Parent Component: beforeCreate
Parent Component: created
Parent Component: beforeMount
Child Component: beforeCreate
Child Component: created
Child Component: beforeMount
Child Component: mounted
Parent Component: mounted
```

- **When toggling the "Toggle Child" button:**
```
Parent Component: beforeUpdate
Child Component: beforeUnmount
Child Component: unmounted
Parent Component: updated
```

This output shows the order in which the lifecycle hooks are executed, both when the page loads and when the child component is conditionally unmounted. You can see how the parent component's lifecycle methods are called before and after the child component's lifecycle methods.

Exercises:

- **Create a simple component with a** `created` **hook that fetches data from an API and updates its** `data` **property.**
- **Create a component with a** `mounted` **hook that adds an event listener**

to a button element.
- **Create a component with a** `beforeUnmount` **hook that cancels the event.**

Fetching Data on Page Load

In the last few sections, we learned how to fetch data from an API endpoint. We created a method called `getPosts` and used Axios to fetch the data. This fetched data, which was a list of posts, was assigned to a data property and then displayed in our template using the `v-for` directive. But remember, we were triggering this `getPosts` method by clicking a button. So, every time we clicked that button, the list of 100 posts was fetched and displayed in the browser.

Now, imagine we want this list of posts to load automatically as soon as the page loads in the browser, instead of waiting for a button click. That's what we'll explore In this section.

The `created` Lifecycle Method

To make this happen, we'll use a special technique called a *lifecycle method*. We learned about lifecycle methods in the previous section. These methods are triggered at specific stages of a component's lifecycle.

To fetch data on page load, we'll use the `created` lifecycle method. The `created` method is called as soon as a component is created and before it is mounted to the DOM (Document Object Model).

Let's head back to our VS Code editor and update our `PostList` component. Inside the component definition, we'll add the `created` method. Remember, the `created` method should be a traditional function, not an arrow function, because arrow functions don't bind the `this` keyword correctly, and this can lead to errors.

```
<template>
  <div>
    <h1>Posts</h1>
    <ul>
      <li v-for="post in posts" :key="post.id">
        {{ post.title }}
      </li>
    </ul>
  </div>
```

```
</template>

<script>
import axios from 'axios';

export default {
  name: 'PostList',
  data() {
    return {
      posts: [],
    };
  },
  created() {
    this.getPosts();
  },
  methods: {
    getPosts() {
      axios.get('https://your-api-endpoint.com/posts')
        .then((response) => {
          this.posts = response.data;
        })
        .catch((error) => {
          console.error(error);
        });
    },
  },
};
</script>
```

In the `created` method, we simply call our `getPosts` method. We can now comment out the button we used before to trigger the data fetch, since it's no longer needed.

Save this code and refresh your browser. You'll see that the list of posts now appears automatically, without needing any user interaction. It's loaded right as the page finishes loading!

We just learned how to leverage the `created` lifecycle method to fetch data on page load. This is a common practice in web applications. Lifecycle methods provide a powerful way to control the behavior of your Vue components at various stages of their existence.

Template Refs

They're a cool way to directly access elements in your Vue app's DOM. Think of it like a way to grab a specific piece of HTML from your template and work with it directly.

One common use case is focusing text inputs. You know, like when you visit a website, and the username field is already highlighted, ready for you to start typing? We can do that using template refs!

Let's build a simple example.

First, we'll create a new file called `TemplateRef.vue` in our `components` folder. You can use the `vbase` snippet (remember that?) to create a basic Vue component.

```
<template>
  <div>
    <input type="text" ref="inputRef">
  </div>
</template>

<script>
export default {
  name: 'TemplateRef',
  mounted() {
    // We'll add code here later
  }
};
</script>
```

In the template, we have a simple input element. We've added a special attribute `ref="inputRef"`. This `ref` attribute is Vue's way of attaching a reference to this input element.

Now, in our `App.vue`, we'll import the `TemplateRef` component:

```
<template>
  <div >
    <TemplateRef />
  </div>
</template>

<script>
import TemplateRef from './components/TemplateRef.vue';

export default {
```

```
  components: {
    TemplateRef
  }
};
</script>
```

If we save and refresh our browser, we'll see the input field.

Let's focus the input when the page loads. To do this, we'll use the `mounted` lifecycle hook in our `TemplateRef` component.

```
<template>
  <div>
    <input type="text" ref="inputRef">
  </div>
</template>

<script>
export default {
  name: 'TemplateRef',
  mounted() {
      // Access the input reference
    this.$refs.inputRef.focus();
  }
};
</script>
```

We access the input element using `this.$refs.inputRef` and call the `focus()` method on it. That's it!

Save and refresh, and our input field will be ready for typing as soon as the page loads.

Refs on Components

You can also attach refs to child components. Let's say we have a `PostList` component we made earlier.

```
<template>
  <div>
    <PostList ref="postListRef"/>
  </div>
</template>

<script>
export default {
  // ... other code

  mounted() {
```

```
      console.log(this.$refs.postListRef);
  }
};
</script>
```

Now, in the `mounted` hook, we can access the `PostList` component instance using `this.$refs.postListRef`.

In summary, template refs provide a way to access DOM elements or child component instances directly within your Vue component. This allows for more dynamic control over your application's behavior.

Exercise:

Let's put this to practice! Modify the `TemplateRef.vue` component to create a button. When the button is clicked, it should change the background color of the input field to yellow. Use a template ref to access the input element and update its style.

Solution:

```
<template>
  <div>
    <input type="text" ref="inputRef">
    <button @click="changeBackgroundColor">Change
Color</button>
  </div>
</template>

<script>
export default {
  // ... other code

  methods: {
    changeBackgroundColor() {
      this.$refs.inputRef.style.backgroundColor = 'yellow';
    }
  }
};
</script>
```

Remember, you can always experiment and try different things. The world of Vue is vast and exciting, and with template refs, you have another powerful tool to make your applications interactive and user-friendly!

Reusability with Mixins

Think of them like reusable chunks of code that you can add to multiple components, keeping things clean and preventing repetition.

Let's start with an example. Imagine we have a simple "Click Counter" component that shows how many times a button is clicked:

```
<template>
  <button @click="incrementCount">Clicked {{ count }}
times</button>
</template>

<script>
export default {
  data() {
    return {
      count: 0,
    };
  },
  methods: {
    incrementCount() {
      this.count++;
    },
  },
};
</script>
```

This component works great! But what if our client now wants a "Hover Counter" that does the same thing but increments when you hover over a heading? We could copy and paste our Click Counter code and change it, but that's not very smart. What if we need ten different counters? We'd be writing the same code over and over!

Here's where Mixins come in. We can extract the core counter logic into a separate file:

Create a `mixins/counter.js` **file:**

```
export default {
  data() {
    return {
      count: 0,
    };
  },
  methods: {
    incrementCount() {
```

```
      this.count++;
    },
  },
};
```

Now, let's use this `counter.js` mixin in both our `Click Counter` and `Hover Counter` components:

Modified `Click Counter`:

```
<template>
  <button @click="incrementCount">Clicked {{ count }}
times</button>
</template>

<script>
import counterMixin from './mixins/counter.js';

export default {
  mixins: [counterMixin],
};
</script>
```

Modified `Hover Counter`:

```
<template>
  <h1 @mouseover="incrementCount">Hovered {{ count }}
times</h1>
</template>

<script>
import counterMixin from './mixins/counter.js';

export default {
  mixins: [counterMixin],
};
</script>
```

Key Steps:

- **Import the Mixin:** We import our `counterMixin` from the `mixins` folder.
- **Remove Duplicated Code:** We remove the `data` and `methods` sections from our component because the mixin provides them.
- **Apply the Mixin:** We add a `mixins` option to our component, which is an array. We put our `counterMixin` inside this array.

Now, both `Click Counter` and `Hover Counter` can use the same counting logic without any code repetition!

Important Points About Mixins:

- **More Than Data and Methods:** Mixins can also include computed properties, watchers, and even lifecycle hooks.
- **Merging with Components:** If a mixin and a component have the same property (like `data`), the component's property takes priority.

Exercise:

Create a new component called `KeyPressCounter` that increments a counter whenever a key is pressed in an input field. Use the `counter.js` mixin to reuse the counter logic.

Solution:

```
<template>
  <div>
    <input type="text" @keyup="incrementCount" />
    <p>Key presses: {{ count }}</p>
  </div>
</template>

<script>
import counterMixin from '../mixins/counter.js';

export default {
  mixins: [counterMixin],
};
</script>
```

Composition API

Now, we're diving into the exciting new addition to Vue 3: the Composition API. It's a powerful tool, but don't worry, we'll break it down step by step.

Think of the Composition API as a new way to write the `script` block within your Vue components. Remember the Options API we've been using? Well, this is a different approach, giving us more flexibility and control.

Let's quickly recap the Options API. We've been using it to build components by configuring options like `data`, `computed`, `methods`, `watch`, and lifecycle hooks. The Composition API offers another way to build components, giving you a choice. Knowing the Options API will make understanding the Composition API much easier, so keep those skills fresh!

So, why did Vue introduce the Composition API? Well, as our Vue projects grow larger and more complex, managing them using the Options API can become challenging. Imagine a huge component with lots of logic spread across different options like `data`, `methods`, and `computed`. It can be difficult to find and understand a specific piece of functionality. Imagine changing a feature and needing to modify code in multiple options – not ideal, right?

Another reason was the difficulty of reusing logic across components. While mixins offered a solution in Vue 2, they weren't perfect. The Composition API addresses these problems by allowing us to encapsulate a specific feature's logic into a single, organized unit. This makes our code more readable and easier to reuse across different components.

Still a little fuzzy? Don't worry. We'll understand it better once we learn how to write components using the Composition API. The best way to learn is by comparing it to the Options API we already know. Think of it as replacing familiar options with their Composition API counterparts.

Replacing data with ref

Now, we're going learn how to replace the `data` option in a Vue component.

We're going to build upon a simple component that uses the data option to store and display a name. Let's imagine our component has a single piece of data, first name, set to "Bruce". We want to use the composition API to achieve the same result.

The Setup

We'll create a new file called DataView.vue in the components folder.

In DataView.vue, we'll define a basic component with the following code:

```
<template>
  <div>
    {{ o_firstName }}
  </div>
</template>

<script>
export default {
  data() {
    return {
      o_firstName: "Bruce"
    }
  }
};
</script>
```

This is our starting point. Now, let's replace the data option with the composition API.

The beauty of Vue 3 is that the options API and the composition API can work together seamlessly within a single component.

To start, we'll add a new method called setup to our Data.vue component. The setup method acts as the entry point for the composition API.

Inside the setup method, we'll use the ref function from Vue to create a reactive reference to a value. Think of it like a container for our data that Vue keeps track of.

We'll import the ref function like this:

```
import { ref } from 'vue';
```

And then use it within our setup method:

```
setup() {
```

```
  const c_firstName = ref("Clark"); // using c_ for
composition api
  return {
    c_firstName
  }
}
```

Now, we've created a reactive reference to a value "Clark" using the `ref` function. Let's break down what's happening here:

- We're storing the reactive reference in a constant called `c_firstName`.
- The `ref` function accepts an initial value, which is "Clark".

You might be thinking, "How do I use this `c_firstName` in my template?".

We need to return an object from the `setup` method, containing the properties we want to expose to our template. In this case, we want to expose `c_firstName`:

```
setup() {
  const c_firstName = ref("Clark");
  return {
    c_firstName
  }
}
```

Finally, we can bind `c_firstName` in the template using the familiar mustache syntax:

```
<template>
  <div>
    {{ c_firstName }}
  </div>
</template>

<script>
import { ref } from 'vue';
export default {
setup() {
  const c_firstName = ref("Clark");
  return {
    c_firstName
  }
}
};
</script>
```

And there you have it! If you run your application, you should see "Clark" rendered instead of "Bruce". We've successfully replaced the `data` option with the composition API!

Let's take a closer look at this `ref` function. `ref` is a function that returns a reactive and mutable object. This object holds a reference to the internal value, making it reactive.

To understand this, we can log `c_firstName` to the console:

```
setup() {
  const c_firstName = ref("Clark");
  console.log(c_firstName);
  return {
    c_firstName
  }
}
```

If you check your browser console, you'll see that the logged value is an object with a `value` property that contains the string "Clark".

This means we can change the value of `c_firstName` by accessing its `value` property:

```
setup() {
  const c_firstName = ref("Clark");
  c_firstName.value = "Diana";
  return {
    c_firstName
  }
}
```

Now, if you refresh your browser, you'll see "Diana" displayed!

While we need to use the `value` property when working with `ref` inside the `setup` method, the template automatically handles it for us. This means you can directly use `c_firstName` within your template without the need for `c_firstName.value`.

Exercise

Let's put what we've learned into practice. Create a new component called `Greeting.vue` and use the `ref` function to store a greeting message. Display the greeting message in your template.

Solution

```
<template>
  <div>
    {{ greeting }}
  </div>
</template>
```

```
<script>
import { ref } from 'vue';

export default {
  setup() {
    const greeting = ref("Hello there!");
    return {
      greeting
    }
  }
};
</script>
```

That's it! We've taken a deep dive into the `ref` function and learned how to replace the `data` option using the composition API.

Replacing data with reactive

We have seen how the `ref` function lets us replace the `data` option in our components. Now, we're going to dive into another powerful function called `reactive` that does the same but in a slightly different way.

We'll use our existing example component with a `data` option that has properties for `firstName`, `lastName`, and `heroName`. This data is already being displayed in our template using the familiar mustache syntax.

Now, let's swap out the `data` option for the `reactive` function. First, we'll import `reactive` from Vue.

```
import { reactive } from 'vue'

export default {
  setup() {
    // ... our code will go here
  }
}
```

Inside the `setup` function, we'll call the `reactive` function. Unlike `ref`, `reactive` takes an object as an argument. We'll include our `firstName`, `lastName`, and `heroName` properties inside this object.

```
setup() {
  const state = reactive({
    firstName: 'Bruce',
    lastName: 'Wayne',
    heroName: 'Batman'
  });
```

```
// ...rest of the code
}
```

Notice how `reactive` returns a reactive reference that we've stored in a constant called `state`. We'll use this `state` to access our data in the template later.

Now, let's build a `greetHero` message using our `state` object.

```
setup() {
  // ...previous code
  const reactiveGreetHero = `Hello ${state.firstName} $
{state.lastName}, also known as ${state.heroName}`;
  return {
    state,
    reactiveGreetHero
  };
}
```

In our template, we'll replace the previous data bindings with the `state` object.

```
<template>
  <div>
    <p>Composition API</p>
    <p>First Name: {{ state.firstName }}</p>
    <p>Last Name: {{ state.lastName }}</p>
    <p>Hero Name: {{ state.heroName }}</p>
    <p>{{ reactiveGreetHero }}</p>
  </div>
</template>
```

If we save and refresh our browser, we'll see the same output as before!

But what have we accomplished? Using `reactive` has allowed us to:

- **Avoid repeating the** `ref` **function** for each property.
- **Eliminate the need for** `dot value` when accessing or modifying our data.

So, when should we use `ref` and when should we use `reactive`?

Here's the rule of thumb:

- `ref`: Use `ref` for primitive types like strings, booleans, and numbers.
- `reactive`: Use `reactive` when you have a group of related primitive types that you want to bundle together as an object.

For example, if we had a component with a `isLoggedIn` property that's a boolean, we'd use `ref` to manage it:

```
setup() {
  const isLoggedIn = ref(false);
  // ...rest of the code
}
```

But if we have properties like firstName, lastName, age, and occupation, we could use reactive to group them into a profile object:

```
setup() {
  const profile = reactive({
    firstName: 'Jane',
    lastName: 'Doe',
    age: 30,
    occupation: 'Software Engineer'
  });
  // ...rest of the code
}
```

This makes our code cleaner and more organized.

We've now learned about two powerful ways to replace the data option in Vue 3 using the composition API: ref and reactive. In the next section, we'll delve into the concept of a reactive reference, which is the backbone of how these functions work, and discover a small improvement we can make to our code.

Reactivity and toRefs

In the last couple of sections, we talked about the ref and reactive functions. We learned that these functions return reactive references which can be stored in constants. But what exactly does that mean? Let's break it down with an example.

Imagine you've got a component called DemoOne.vue where you want to display a name. Using the composition API, you can create a constant called name and set it to "Developer". Then, you return this constant and bind it to the template. You'll see "Developer" displayed on the screen.

In this example we will use <script setup> which is strictly for composition API instead of setup() which is used to use composition API with option API. With <script setup> you do not have to return use return statement.

```
<template>
  <div>
    {{ name }}
```

```
    </div>
</template>

<script setup>
import { ref } from 'vue'

const name = ref('Developer')
</script>
```

So, why do we need the `ref` function? Well, let's say you want to update the `name` property after two seconds. You might try to change the `const` to `let` and use `setTimeout` to update the value.

```
<script setup>
import { ref } from 'vue'

const name = ref('Developer')

setTimeout(() => {
  name = 'Developer's Guide'
}, 2000)
</script>
```

You'll see an error message, "Constant value cannot be changed." But even if you change it to `let`, you'll notice that the name doesn't update on the screen, even though it changes in the console.

This is where `ref` comes in. `ref` tells Vue that the value has changed and the UI needs to update. Let's fix our code by using the `ref` function:

```
<script setup>
import { ref } from 'vue'

const name = ref('Developer')

setTimeout(() => {
  name.value = "Developer's Guide"
}, 2000)
</script>
```

Now, after two seconds, the name on the screen will change to "Developer's Guide". Vue is now reacting to the change in the `name` value and updating the DOM.

The `reactive` function works in a similar way. It allows Vue to track changes in the values of an object and update the UI accordingly.

Let's look at another example. Imagine we have a component `DemoTwo.vue` where we want to display a first name and last name. We can use the `reactive` function to create an object with these properties:

```
<template>
  <div>
    {{ state.firstName }} {{ state.lastName }}
  </div>
</template>

<script setup>
import { reactive } from 'vue'

const state = reactive({
  firstName: 'Bruce',
  lastName: 'Wayne'
})

</script>
```

Notice how we have to access the properties using `state.firstName` and `state.lastName` in the template. This is different from using the `data` option in the options API where we could directly bind the properties as `firstName` and `lastName`.

Luckily, we can use the `toRefs` function to make this easier. The `toRefs` function takes an object and returns a new object where each property is wrapped in a `ref`. Let's update our code:

```
<template>
  <div>
    {{ firstName }} {{ lastName }}
  </div>
</template>

<script setup>
import { reactive, toRefs } from 'vue'

const state = reactive({
  firstName: 'Bruce',
  lastName: 'Wayne'
})

const { firstName, lastName } = toRefs(state)

setTimeout(() => {
  state.firstName = 'Clark'
  state.lastName = 'Kent'
}, 2000)
</script>
```

Now, when we update the `firstName` and `lastName` properties in the `state` object after two seconds, the UI will update to "Clark Kent". The `toRefs` function ensures that Vue keeps track of changes in the individual properties.

So, in this section, we learned about the reactivity feature in Vue and how the `ref`, `reactive`, and `toRefs` functions work together to make our UI dynamic and responsive. In the next section, we'll explore how to replace the `methods` option using the composition API.

Methods

In previous sections, we have seen how to replace the `data` option in our Vue 3 components with the composition API. Now, let's tackle another common component element: the `methods` option.

Imagine you're building a simple counter. You've got your trusty `data` option to hold the count, and you want a button to increment it. Here's how you might write it in a traditional Vue 2 way:

```
<template>
  <div>
    <p>Count: {{ count }}</p>
    <button @click="incrementCount">Increment</button>
  </div>
</template>

<script>
export default {
  data() {
    return {
      count: 0
    };
  },
  methods: {
    incrementCount() {
      this.count++;
    }
  }
};
</script>
```

This code defines a component with a `count` variable, a button to trigger the `incrementCount` function, and the `incrementCount` function itself within the `methods` option. Easy, right?

But the composition API provides a more organized way to manage our component's logic. Instead of having our data and methods scattered throughout the component, the composition API allows us to group related functionalities together.

Let's replace our `methods` option with the composition API. We'll start by importing the `ref` function from Vue:

```
<script>
import { ref } from 'vue';

export default {
  setup() {
    const count = ref(0);

    const incrementCount = () => {
      count.value++;
    };

    return { count, incrementCount };
  }
};
</script>
```

or with `<script setup>`:

```
<script setup>
import { ref } from 'vue';
    const count = ref(0);

    const incrementCount = () => {
      count.value++;
    };
</script>
```

In this code, we define our `count` variable using the `ref` function, which allows us to track changes. We then define our `incrementCount` function within the `setup` method and increment the `count.value`. We're also returning both the `count` and `incrementCount` functions so they're accessible within our template.

Now, how do we use these in our template? Simple! Just use the returned variables:

```
<template>
  <div>
    <p>Count: {{ count }}</p>
    <button @click="incrementCount">Increment</button>
  </div>
```

```
</template>
```

Now when we click the "Increment" button, our count will update!

But wait, there's more! What if we want to manage multiple pieces of data? We can use the `reactive` function to create reactive objects. Let's modify our counter example to have a name property as well:

```
<script>
import { ref, reactive } from 'vue';

export default {
  setup() {
    const state = reactive({
      count: 0,
      name: 'Alice'
    });

    const incrementCount = () => {
      state.count++;
    };

    const changeName = () => {
      state.name = 'Bob';
    };

    return { state, incrementCount, changeName };
  }
};
</script>
```

We've now created a `state` object using the `reactive` function. This means any changes to the properties within `state` will trigger a re-render of our component. We can now easily access and manipulate our `count` and `name` properties within our functions.

In our template, we can bind the `count` and `name` properties to display them:

```
<template>
  <div>
    <p>Count: {{ state.count }}</p>
    <p>Name: {{ state.name }}</p>
    <button @click="incrementCount">Increment Count</button>
    <button @click="changeName">Change Name</button>
  </div>
</template>
```

Now when we click "Increment Count," our count will increase, and when we click "Change Name," our name will change to "Bob."

The composition API allows you to group related functionality together, making your components more maintainable and easier to understand. As you become more comfortable with the composition API, you'll see even more benefits to this approach.

Exercise:

Let's put our new knowledge to the test. Create a simple component that displays a message and has a button to change the message. The initial message should be "Hello, world!" and the button should change it to "Goodbye, world!" Use the `reactive` function and the composition API to manage your data and methods.

Solution:

```
<template>
  <div>
    <p>{{ state.message }}</p>
    <button @click="changeMessage">Change Message</button>
  </div>
</template>

<script>
import { reactive } from 'vue';

export default {
  setup() {
    const state = reactive({
      message: 'Hello, world!'
    });

    const changeMessage = () => {
      state.message = 'Goodbye, world!';
    };

    return { state, changeMessage };
  }
};
</script>
```

v-model

Our next step is to understand how the Composition API works with the v-model directive. To get started, create VModel.vue in the components folder within our project. It should contains a `data` option with two properties, `fname` and `lname`. In the template, we have two input elements and we use the `v-model` directive with the `fname` and `lname` properties for two-way binding.

```
<template>
  <div>
     <p>{{ fname }} - {{ lname }}</p>
     <input type="text" v-model="fname" />
     <input type="text" v-model="lname" />
  </div>
</template>

<script>
export default {
  data() {
    return {
      fname: "",
      lname: "",
    };
  },
};
</script>
```

If we include this component in `App.vue` and head to the browser, we'll see both input fields. Now, let's verify the working of the `v-model` directive. At the moment, you'll see they have empty strings as values. If you type "David Stone" into the input fields, you'll see those values reflected above the input fields. This shows our binding from the view to the model is working as expected.

Now, let's understand the same thing using the Composition API. By now, you should have a good understanding of the `ref` and `reactive` functions from Vue. So, I'm going to tackle both of them at the same time.

In the script block, import `ref`, `reactive`, and `toRefs` from Vue. Next, add the `setup` method. Within the method, let's store values using both the `ref` and `reactive` functions.

```
<script>
import { ref, reactive, toRefs } from "vue";

export default {
  setup() {
    const heroName = ref("");
    const state = reactive({
      firstName: "",
```

```
        lastName: "",
    });

    return { heroName, ...toRefs(state) };
  },
};
</script>
```

Here, `heroName` is an empty string to begin with. We also have `state` which is an object with `firstName` and `lastName` properties, both initially empty strings. We return both of these so we can use them in the template.

Now, we can add the input elements in the template and use `v-model` for two-way binding.

```
<template>
  <div>
    <input type="text" v-model="heroName" />
    <input type="text" v-model="firstName" />
    <input type="text" v-model="lastName" />
  </div>
</template>
```

As you can see with the `v-model` directive, we don't have to unpack the value from the `heroName` reference; we can directly use the constant. The `reactive` approach is also straightforward.

Let's save the file, head back to the browser, and ensure everything works as expected.

On page load, we have the three input elements. In the developer tools, you'll see the properties under a `setup` section. If you type "Hero Name" into the first input field, you'll see the same value updated in the developer tools. Next, update the "First Name" and "Last Name" inputs, and you can see those values reflected at the top of the input fields. Our `v-model` directive with the Composition API is working as expected.

As you can see, the template remains the same whether we use the Options API or the Composition API.

Exercise: Modify the code to add a fourth input field using the `reactive` approach and bind it to a new property called `email` in the `state` object.

Solution:

```
<template>
  <div>
    <input type="text" v-model="heroName" />
```

```
      <input type="text" v-model="firstName" />
      <input type="text" v-model="lastName" />
      <input type="text" v-model="email" />
    </div>
</template>

<script>
import { ref, reactive, toRefs } from "vue";

export default {
  setup() {
    const heroName = ref("");
    const state = reactive({
      firstName: "",
      lastName: "",
      email: "",
    });

    return { heroName, ...toRefs(state) };
  },
};
</script>
```

Computed Properties

In this section, we'll explore how to replace the computed property option with the Composition API in Vue JS 3. This technique allows us to write more organized and reusable code, especially when working with complex components.

Let's start with a basic example. Imagine we have a simple component with two input fields for first name and last name, and we want to display the full name as a computed value. In our previous code, we would use the computed option within the component to achieve this.

```
<template>
  <div>
    <input type="text" v-model="fname" />
    <input type="text" v-model="lname" />
    <p>Full Name: {{ fullName }}</p>
  </div>
</template>

<script>
export default {
  data() {
    return {
```

```
      fname: '',
      lname: '',
    };
  },
  computed: {
    fullName() {
      return this.fname + ' ' + this.lname;
    },
  },
};
</script>
```

In this example, the `fullName` property is calculated whenever `fname` or `lname` changes, thanks to the `computed` option. Now, let's see how to achieve the same functionality using the Composition API.

Using `ref`

First, we'll import the `ref` function from Vue:

```
import { ref, computed } from 'vue';
```

Next, within the `setup` function, we create two references using `ref`:

```
const refFirstName = ref('');
const refLastName = ref('');
```

These references will hold the values for first name and last name. We can then bind these references to the input fields using the `v-model` directive:

```
<template>
  <div>
    <input type="text" v-model="refFirstName" />
    <input type="text" v-model="refLastName" />
    <p>Full Name: {{ refFullName }}</p>
  </div>
</template>
```

To calculate the full name, we use the `computed` function from Vue. This function accepts a function that returns the computed value. Here's how it looks:

```
const refFullName = computed(() => {
  return refFirstName.value + ' ' + refLastName.value;
});
```

Finally, we return the `refFullName` along with the references from the `setup` function:

```
setup() {
const refFirstName = ref('');
const refLastName = ref('');
```

```
const refFullName = computed(() => {
  return refFirstName.value + ' ' + refLastName.value;
});
  return {
    refFirstName,
    refLastName,
    refFullName,
  };
}
```

Using reactive

We can also use the reactive function to create reactive data objects. This approach is useful when we have multiple related properties.

```
import { reactive, computed } from 'vue';
```

Within the setup function, we define a reactive object with our properties:

```
const state = reactive({
  reactiveFirstName: '',
  reactiveLastName: '',
});
```

We then bind these properties to the input fields:

```
<template>
  <div>
    <input type="text" v-model="state.reactiveFirstName" />
    <input type="text" v-model="state.reactiveLastName" />
    <p>Full Name: {{ reactiveFullName }}</p>
  </div>
</template>
```

The computed function is used to calculate the full name using the reactive properties:

```
const reactiveFullName = computed(() => {
  return state.reactiveFirstName + ' ' +
state.reactiveLastName;
});
```

Finally, we return the reactiveFullName and the state object from the setup function:

```
setup() {
const state = reactive({
  reactiveFirstName: '',
  reactiveLastName: '',
});
const reactiveFullName = computed(() => {
  return state.reactiveFirstName + ' ' +
state.reactiveLastName;
```

```
});
  return {
    state,
    reactiveFullName,
  };
}
```

Key Points

- When using `ref`, you need to access the value of a reference using the `.value` property.
- When using `reactive`, you can directly access the properties of the reactive object.
- Remember to return both the computed value and the references or reactive object from the `setup` function.
- Vue will automatically update the computed value whenever the underlying references or reactive properties change.

Exercise:

Create a component with two input fields for first name and age. Display the user's full name and age, using the Composition API to compute the full name.

Solution:

```
<template>
  <div>
    <input type="text" v-model="firstName" />
    <input type="number" v-model="age" />
    <p>Full Name: {{ fullName }}</p>
    <p>Age: {{ age }}</p>
  </div>
</template>

<script>
import { ref, computed } from 'vue';

export default {
  setup() {
    const firstName = ref('');
    const age = ref(0);

    const fullName = computed(() => {
      return firstName.value + ' (Age: ' + age.value + ')';
    });

    return {
```

```
      firstName,
      age,
      fullName,
    };
  },
};
</script>
```

By replacing the `computed` option with the Composition API, we can write more modular and reusable code. The Composition API provides flexibility and allows us to organize our logic in a structured way.

Watchers

So, we're going to replace the "watch" option with the composition API.

Let's start with a basic component. Imagine we have a text input where users can enter their name. We want to track every change in this name input and print it to the console. We'll use the "watch" option to do this.

```
<template>
  <div>
    <input type="text" v-model="name" />
  </div>
</template>

<script>
export default {
  data() {
    return {
      name: '',
    };
  },
  watch: {
    name(newValue, oldValue) {
      console.log('New Value:', newValue);
      console.log('Old Value:', oldValue);
    },
  },
};
</script>
```

In this code, we have a simple component with an input field. The `v-model` directive binds the `name` data property to the input. The `watch` option contains a property called `name` that triggers a function when the `name` property changes. This function logs the new and old values of the `name` property.

Moving to the Composition API

Now, let's replace this "watch" option with the composition API. We'll do this in a few steps:

Import ref **and** watch**:** We'll need to import the ref and watch functions from Vue.

```
import { ref, watch } from 'vue';
```

Define the Setup Method: We'll add a new method called setup to our component.

```
setup() {
  // Our code will go here
}
```

Use ref**:** The ref function allows us to create a reactive variable. Instead of using the data option, we'll create a reference to our name variable.

```
setup() {
  const firstName = ref(''); // Create a ref for our name

  return {
    firstName, // Make it available in the template
  };
}
```

Bind in the Template: We'll use the v-model directive to bind the firstName ref to our input field.

```
<template>
  <div>
    <input type="text" v-model="firstName" />
  </div>
</template>
```

Watch the Ref: Now, within the setup method, we'll use the watch function to monitor changes to our firstName ref.

```
setup() {
  const firstName = ref(''); // Create a ref for our name
  watch(firstName, (newValue, oldValue) => {
    console.log('New Value:', newValue);
    console.log('Old Value:', oldValue);
  });

  return {
    firstName, // Make it available in the template
  };
```

```
}
```

Watching Multiple Sources

Sometimes, you might want to react to changes in multiple data sources.
Let's say we have another ref called `lastName`. We can modify the `watch`
function to observe changes to both `firstName` and `lastName`:

```
setup() {
  // ... (previous code)

  const lastName = ref('Wayne'); // New ref

  watch([firstName, lastName], (newValues, oldValues) => {
    console.log('New First Name:', newValues[0]);
    console.log('Old First Name:', oldValues[0]);
    console.log('New Last Name:', newValues[1]);
    console.log('Old Last Name:', oldValues[1]);
  });

  // ... (return statement)
}
```

Now, our `watch` function will execute whenever either `firstName` or
`lastName` changes.

Immediate Watchers

By default, the watcher function is only executed when a value changes.
But what if we want it to run immediately when the component is loaded?
We can use the `immediate` option:

```
setup() {
  // ... (previous code)

  watch(firstName, (newValue, oldValue) => {
    // ...
  }, { immediate: true }); // Add the third argument

  // ... (return statement)
}
```

Exercise:

Create a component that tracks changes to a user's age. Use the
composition API and make sure the watcher logs the changes to the
console.

Solution:

```
<template>
  <div>
    <input type="number" v-model="age" />
  </div>
</template>

<script>
import { ref, watch } from 'vue';

export default {
  setup() {
    const age = ref(0); // Initialize age to 0

    watch(age, (newValue, oldValue) => {
      console.log('New Age:', newValue);
      console.log('Old Age:', oldValue);
    });

    return {
      age,
    };
  },
};
</script>
```

This component creates a ref for the age, binds it to an input field, and uses the watch function to log changes to the age.

Watching reactive data

In the last section, we learned how to use the composition API to replace the watch option. We looked at how to watch data created with the ref function. Now, let's dive into the differences when using the watch API with reactive functions.

We'll start by importing reactive from Vue. We also need two refs for the return statement, so we'll import that as well.

```
import { toRefs, reactive } from 'vue';
```

Now, let's call the reactive function and pass in an object. We'll create a state object with two properties: fname and lname, both initially set to empty strings.

```
const state = reactive({
  fname: '',
```

```
    lname: ''
});
```

We'll return `state` using the `refs` function and spread it to create our refs.

```
return {
    ...toRefs(state)
};
```

In our template, we'll bind `fname` and `lname` to input elements using the `v-model` directive. We'll also update the placeholder text for clarity.

```
<template>
  <div>
    <input type="text" placeholder="Reactive First Name" v-model="fname">
    <input type="text" placeholder="Reactive Last Name" v-model="lname">
  </div>
</template>
```

Now, let's add the watcher for this reactive reference. We use the `watch` function, which takes two arguments. The first argument is the data source, which is `state`. The second argument is the function to be executed when one of the `state` properties changes.

```
watch(state, (newValue, oldValue) => {
  console.log('fname old value:', oldValue.fname);
  console.log('fname new value:', newValue.fname);
  console.log('lname old value:', oldValue.lname);
  console.log('lname new value:', newValue.lname);
});
```

When we run this code, you'll see that the old and new values for both `fname` and `lname` are the same, even when we type in the input fields. This is because the `reactive` function returns a proxy object that intercepts property access and updates the underlying data. It's designed to work with reactive objects, so it updates the internal state directly without triggering the `watch` function to display old and new values separately.

So, how do we access the old values? We can use a getter function to provide a copy of the object's values instead of the reactive object itself. We'll update the first argument of our `watch` function to return an object with the spread values of `state`.

```
watch(() => ({...state}), (newValue, oldValue) => {
  console.log('fname old value:', oldValue.fname);
  console.log('fname new value:', newValue.fname);
  console.log('lname old value:', oldValue.lname);
  console.log('lname new value:', newValue.lname);
```

```
});
```

Now, we can see the old and new values as we type in the input fields. This is because the `watch` function now receives a fresh copy of the object for each change, so the old and new values are distinct.

However, if we have many properties in our reactive object, having the same function execute for every change can be inefficient. Let's add a watcher specifically for the `fname` property.

```
watch(state.fname, (newValue, oldValue) => {
  console.log('fname old value:', oldValue);
  console.log('fname new value:', newValue);
});
```

This will only trigger when the `fname` property changes. But when we try to run this code, we encounter a warning: "Invalid watch source". This is because individual properties in a reactive object also need to be accessed through a getter function. We'll update the first argument of our `watch` function to return `state.fname` inside an arrow function.

```
watch(() => state.fname, (newValue, oldValue) => {
  console.log('fname old value:', oldValue);
  console.log('fname new value:', newValue);
});
```

Now, our `watch` function only triggers when `fname` changes, and we can see the old and new values.

Lastly, we'll explore deep watchers. Let's add a nested object `options` to our reactive `state` with a property `heroName`.

```
const state = reactive({
  fname: '',
  lname: '',
  options: {
    heroName: ''
  }
});
```

We'll bind `options.heroName` to another input element in our template.

```
<template>
  <div>
    <input type="text" placeholder="Reactive Hero Name" v-model="options.heroName">
  </div>
</template>
```

Now, if we try to watch the `options` object, we won't see any log statements when we type in the `heroName` field. This is because `watch` only observes changes to the top level of the object. To monitor changes within nested objects, we need to set the `deep` option to `true`.

```
watch(() => state.options, (newValue, oldValue) => {
  console.log('options old value:', oldValue);
  console.log('options new value:', newValue);
}, { deep: true });
```

With `deep: true`, we can see the old and new values for the `options` object. But, just like before, the old and new values are the same because `watch` is comparing the entire object, which is essentially a proxy object, and will always show the same for both values. To get around this, we need to make a deep copy of the `options` object.

We'll use the `cloneDeep` function from the `lodash` library to create a deep copy. First, install `lodash` using the command `npm install lodash`. Then, import `lodash` and use the `cloneDeep` function in our `watch` function.

```
import { ref, reactive } from 'vue';
import { cloneDeep } from 'lodash';

// ... code

watch(() => cloneDeep(state.options), (newValue, oldValue)
=> {
  console.log('options old value:', oldValue);
  console.log('options new value:', newValue);
}, { deep: true });
```

Now, we can see the old and new values separately when we type in the `heroName` field, as we're working with independent copies of the `options` object for both `oldValue` and `newValue`.

To watch the value inside the 'options', you do not need lodash. Simply do this:

```
watch(() => state.options.heroName, (newValue, oldValue) =>
{
  console.log('options old value:', oldValue);
  console.log('options new value:', newValue);
}, { deep: true });
```

That concludes our discussion on using the `watch` function with reactive objects and the `deep` option for nested properties.

Provide/Inject

Let's get into replacing the `provide` and `inject` options API with the Composition API!

You might recall that `provide` and `inject` allow us to pass data from a parent component to a deeply nested child without passing props through every intermediate component.

Let's say we have a parent component named `ProvideInject` that holds a data property called `name` set to "Developer". We have nested components `ChildA`, `ChildB`, and `ChildC`, with `ChildC` being the deepest nested. Using `provide` and `inject`, we can share the `name` value from `ProvideInject` to `ChildC` directly.

```
<template>
  <div>
    Parent component: {{ name }}
    <ChildA />
  </div>
</template>

<script>
import ChildA from "./ChildA.vue";

export default {
  components: { ChildA },
  data() {
    return {
      name: "Developer",
    };
  },
};
</script>
```

ChildA:
```
<template>
  <div>
    Child A component
    <ChildB />
  </div>
</template>

<script>
import ChildB from "./ChildB.vue";

export default {
```

```
  components: { ChildB },
};
</script>
```

ChildB:
```
<template>
  <div>
    Child B component
    <ChildC />
  </div>
</template>

<script>
import ChildC from "./ChildC.vue";

export default {
  components: { ChildC },
};
</script>
```

ChildC:
```
<template>
  <div>
    Child C component: {{ username }}
  </div>
</template>

<script>
import { inject } from "vue";

export default {
};
</script>
```

In our `ProvideInject` component, let's add a new data property called `c_username` and provide it as a static string:

```
<script>
import { provide } from "vue";

export default {
  setup() {
    const username = ref("Developer's Guide");
    provide("c_username", username);
    return {};
  },
};
</script>
```

In `ChildC`, we'll inject this value:

```
<script>
import { inject } from "vue";

export default {
  setup() {
    const username = inject("c_username", "Default
Username");
    return { username };
  },
};
</script>
```

And in the template:

```
<template>
  <div>
    Child C component: {{ username }}
  </div>
</template>
```

Now, when we refresh the browser, we should see "Developer's Guide" in ChildC! If we remove the provide line in ProvideInject, the default value "Default Username" will be displayed.

Providing and Injecting Reactive Values

Let's move on to working with reactive values using ref and reactive. We'll update ProvideInject to define reactive values:

```
<script>
import { provide, ref, reactive } from "vue";

export default {
  setup() {
    const count = ref(0);
    const state = reactive({
      firstName: "Bruce",
      lastName: "Wayne",
    });

    provide("c_count", count);
    provide("c_hero", state);

    return { count, ...state };
  },
};
</script>
```

And we'll inject them in ChildC:

```
<script>
import { inject, ref } from "vue";

export default {
  setup() {
    const childCount = inject("c_count", 0);
    const childHero = inject("c_hero", {});

    return { childCount, ...childHero };
  },
};
</script>
```

In the templates, we can now bind these values:

```
<!-- ProvideInject component -->
<template>
  <div>
    Parent component count: {{ count }}
    Parent component hero: {{ state.firstName }}
{{ state.lastName }}
  </div>
</template>
```

```
<!-- ChildC component -->
<template>
  <div>
    Child C component count: {{ childCount }}
    Child C component hero: {{ childHero.firstName }}
{{ childHero.lastName }}
  </div>
</template>
```

Updating Values and Change Handlers

You'll typically update reactive values in the parent component and not directly in the child. Let's demonstrate that by adding an increment button in ProvideInject and providing the click handler to ChildC:

```
<!-- ProvideInject component -->
<template>
  <div>
    <button @click="incrementCount">Increment Count</button>
  </div>
</template>

<script>
import { provide, ref, reactive } from "vue";

export default {
```

```
setup() {
  const count = ref(0);
  const state = reactive({
    firstName: "Bruce",
    lastName: "Wayne",
  });

  provide("c_count", count);
  provide("c_hero", state);
  provide("incrementCount", incrementCount);

  const incrementCount = () => {
    count.value++;
  };

  return { count, ...state, incrementCount };
},
};
</script>
```

In ChildC, we inject the incrementCount function:

```
<script>
import { inject, ref } from "vue";

export default {
  setup() {
    const childCount = inject("c_count", 0);
    const childHero = inject("c_hero", {});
    const incrementCount = inject("incrementCount");

    return { childCount, ...childHero, incrementCount };
  },
};
</script>
```

And add a button that calls this function:

```
<template>
  <button @click="incrementCount">Increment Count from
Child</button>
</template>
```

Now, clicking either button will increment the count value in both the parent and child components!

Recap

- The provide function accepts a label and value.
- The inject function accepts a label and an optional default value.
- Always return injected values from the setup method and bind them to

the template.

That's the basics of replacing `provide` and `inject` with the Composition API!

Lifecycle Hooks

"What are lifecycle hooks, and why should I care?" Well, picture this: your Vue component is like a tiny little person going through different stages of life. Lifecycle hooks are like events that happen at each stage, giving you a chance to do something special.

For example, you can use a lifecycle hook to grab some data from the server *before* the component is displayed on the screen. Or maybe you want to change something on the screen *after* the component is fully ready.

We've already talked about these lifecycle hooks in a previous section, so if you haven't seen that one, make sure to check it out first.

Here's the thing: the **composition API** has changed the way we use these lifecycle hooks a little. But don't worry, it's not that complicated!

In the **options API**, you had a bunch of options to set up your component. One of those options was the `beforeCreate` lifecycle hook. You'd just add a function to that option, and Vue would run it before the component was created.

With the **composition API**, things are a bit more organized. The `beforeCreate` and `created` lifecycle hooks have been **merged** into the `setup` method, which you're already familiar with.

Now, for the rest of the hooks, things are super simple. Vue has just added an **"on"** prefix to their names. So, `beforeMount` becomes `onBeforeMount`, `mounted` becomes `onMounted`, and so on.

Let me show you how this looks in code:

LifecycleO.vue:

```
<template>
  <div>
    {{ message }}
  </div>
</template>
```

```
<script>
export default {
  data() {
    return {
      message: 'Hello from Lifecycle0.vue!',
    };
  },
  beforeCreate() {
    console.log('Lifecycle0: beforeCreate');
  },
  created() {
    console.log('Lifecycle0: created');
  },
  beforeMount() {
    console.log('Lifecycle0: beforeMount');
  },
  mounted() {
    console.log('Lifecycle0: mounted');
  },
  beforeUpdate() {
    console.log('Lifecycle0: beforeUpdate');
  },
  updated() {
    console.log('Lifecycle0: updated');
  },
  beforeUnmount() {
    console.log('Lifecycle0: beforeUnmount');
  },
  unmounted() {
    console.log('Lifecycle0: unmounted');
  },
};
</script>
```

LifecycleC.vue:

```
<template>
  <div>
    {{ message }}
  </div>
</template>

<script>
import {
  onBeforeMount,
  onMounted,
  onBeforeUpdate,
  onUpdated,
  onBeforeUnmount,
  onUnmounted
```

```
} from 'vue';

export default {
  setup() {
    const message = 'Hello from LifecycleC.vue!';

    onBeforeMount(() => {
      console.log('LifecycleC: onBeforeMount');
    });

    onMounted(() => {
      console.log('LifecycleC: onMounted');
    });

    onBeforeUpdate(() => {
      console.log('LifecycleC: onBeforeUpdate');
    });

    onUpdated(() => {
      console.log('LifecycleC: onUpdated');
    });

    onBeforeUnmount(() => {
      console.log('LifecycleC: onBeforeUnmount');
    });

    onUnmounted(() => {
      console.log('LifecycleC: onUnmounted');
    });

    return { message };
  },
};
</script>
```

Let's break down what's happening:

In **LifecycleO.vue**, we have the traditional options API approach. We define all the lifecycle hooks as options within the component. When the component goes through its lifecycle, these functions will be called at the appropriate time.

In **LifecycleC.vue**, we're using the composition API. We import the lifecycle hooks from Vue and then call them within the setup method. Each lifecycle hook is passed a function that will be executed at the right moment.

Template Refs

Earlier, we learned about Template Refs, which are awesome for directly interacting with DOM elements within your Vue component. Think of them as a way to grab a specific part of your website's building blocks. We used this to focus an input element as soon as the page loaded.

Let's recap! Imagine we have a simple input field on our page. We want to make sure the cursor is blinking inside it, ready for the user to type. That's where Template Refs come in!

```html
<template>
  <input type="text" ref="inputRef" />
</template>
```

We've added a `ref="inputRef"` attribute to our input. This gives us a handy reference point to access this element within our JavaScript code.

```javascript
<script>
import { ref, onMounted } from 'vue';

export default {
  setup() {
    const inputRef = ref(null);

    // When the component loads
    onMounted(() => {
      // Focus the input
      inputRef.value.focus();
    });

    return { inputRef };
  },
};
</script>
```

Using the `ref()` function from Vue, we create a reactive reference called `inputRef`. This lets us track changes to the input element. The `onMounted` lifecycle hook is triggered when the component is fully loaded, allowing us to use `inputRef.value.focus()` to set the focus on the input.

Notice how we return `inputRef` from our `setup` function. This makes it available to use within our template.

Exercise:

Let's try something different. Instead of focusing on page load, create a button that focuses the input element when clicked.

Solution:

```
<template>
  <input type="text" ref="inputRef" />
  <button @click="focusInput">Focus Input</button>
</template>
<script>
import { ref } from 'vue';

export default {
  setup() {
    const inputRef = ref(null);

    const focusInput = () => {
      inputRef.value.focus();
    };

    return { inputRef, focusInput };
  },
};
</script>
```

Props

In this section, we'll learn how to use props with the Composition API in Vue.js.

First, we'll create two files within the `components` folder: `PersonView.vue` and `PersonGreeting.vue`. `PersonView.vue` will be our parent component, and `PersonGreeting.vue` will be the child component.

Inside `PersonView.vue`, we'll have two input fields for first name and last name. These will be bound to reactive values using the `ref` function. This means our `person` component is built entirely with the Composition API.

```
<template>
  <div>
    <input type="text" v-model="firstName.value"
placeholder="First Name">
    <input type="text" v-model="lastName.value"
placeholder="Last Name">
    <person-greeting :first-name="firstName.value" :last-
name="lastName.value" />
  </div>
</template>

<script>
import { ref } from 'vue';
```

```
import PersonGreeting from
'./components/PersonGreeting.vue';

export default {
  components: {
    PersonGreeting,
  },
  setup() {
    const firstName = ref('');
    const lastName = ref('');

    return {
      firstName,
      lastName,
    };
  },
};
</script>
```

In the component's template, we also include the `PersonGreeting` component. We'll pass the `firstName` and `lastName` as props to this component.

Now, let's create `PersonGreeting.vue`. This component, as the name suggests, will render a greeting message using the passed-in props.

```
<template>
  <p>Hello, {{ firstName }} {{ lastName }}!</p>
</template>

<script>
export default {
  props: {
    firstName: String,
    lastName: String,
  },
};
</script>
```

The `personGreeting` component receives `firstName` and `lastName` as props, which are then bound to the template using the mustache syntax.

If we include `person.vue` in our `App.vue` component and run our application, we should see two input fields and the greeting message from the child component. As we type in the input fields, the greeting message will update accordingly.

However, even though our child component works perfectly, there's a better way to define our template. Instead of using separate `firstName` and `lastName` props, we can combine them into a single computed property. Let's see how to do this first with the Options API and then with the Composition API.

Options API:

In `personGreeting.vue`, we'll add a computed option. This option is an object, and our computed property will be called `fullName`.

```
<script>
export default {
  props: {
    firstName: String,
    lastName: String,
  },
  computed: {
    fullName() {
      return `${this.firstName} ${this.lastName}`;
    },
  },
};
</script>
```

Inside the `fullName` function, we simply return the concatenation of `firstName` and `lastName`. Now, in our template, we can bind just `fullName`.

```
<template>
  <p>Hello, {{ fullName }}!</p>
</template>
```

If we refresh our browser and fill in the inputs with "David Stone," we'll still see the same output.

Composition API:

Now, let's replace the Options API computed option with the Composition API's `computed` function.

```
<script>
import { computed } from 'vue';

export default {
  props: {
    firstName: String,
    lastName: String,
  },
  setup(props) {
```

```
    const fullName = computed(() => {
      return `${props.firstName} ${props.lastName}`;
    });

    return {
      fullName,
    };
  },
};
</script>
```

First, we import the `computed` function from Vue. Then, within the `setup` method, we define our `fullName` computed property. This property is assigned the result of the `computed` function, which takes another function as an argument. Inside this function, we return the concatenation of `firstName` and `lastName`.

Remember, the `setup` method is called early in the component's lifecycle, so `this` won't point to the component instance, and will be `undefined`. However, the `setup` method receives an argument, which is the `props` object for this component. This is how we access the `firstName` and `lastName` values within the computed function.

Finally, we return the `fullName` property from the `setup` method so that our template binding works correctly. If we refresh our browser, fill in "Clark Kent," and our UI still functions as expected.

So, when using the Composition API, if you need to access the component props, they are available as the first argument to the `setup` method. Or use <script setup> which is recommended for Composition API if you have no intention of using options API:

```
<script setup>
import { computed, defineProps } from 'vue';

const props = defineProps (
  {
    firstName: String,
    lastName: String,
  } )

    const fullName = computed(() => {
      return `${props.firstName} ${props.lastName}`;
    });

</script>
```

This is how we can pass information from the parent component to the child component.

In the next section, we'll explore how to pass information from the child component back to the parent – that is, emitting events from the child to the parent using the Composition API. Stay tuned!

Custom Events

In this section, we're diving into custom events and how they interact with the Composition API. Imagine you have a child component that needs to send information back to its parent. That's where custom events shine! We'll use a simple example to illustrate this concept.

Let's consider two components: Person (the parent) and PersonGreeting (the child). We'll create a button within the PersonGreeting component. When clicked, it'll send a custom event to the Person component with some information, and then display an alert with that information.

The Child Component (PersonGreeting.vue)

```
<template>
  <button @click="sendEvent">Call Heroes</button>
</template>

<script>
import { ref } from 'vue';

export default {
  setup(props, context) {
    const fullName = ref('David Stone');

    const sendEvent = () => {
      context.emit('callHeroes', fullName.value);
    };

    return {
      sendEvent,
      fullName
    };
  }
};
</script>
```

Or use <script setup> which is recommended for Composition API if you have no intention of using options API:

```
<script setup>
import { ref, defineEmits } from 'vue';
const fullName = ref('David Stone');
const emits = defineEmits (['callHeroes'])

    const sendEvent = () => {
      emits('callHeroes', fullName.value);
    };

</script>
```

The Parent Component (Person.vue**)**

```
<template>
  <PersonGreeting @callHeroes="callHeroes" />
</template>

<script>
import PersonGreeting from
'./components/PersonGreeting.vue';

export default {
  components: {
    PersonGreeting,
  },
  setup() {
    const callHeroes = (hero) => {
      alert(`Calling ${hero}`);
    };

    return {
      callHeroes
    };
  }
};
</script>
```

After running this code, you'll see a button that says "Call Heroes" on the page. When you click the button, an alert message will pop up saying "Calling David Stone."

Key Takeaway: The `context` object provided as the second argument in the `setup` method is a powerful tool that exposes several important methods, including `emit`, `slots`, and `attrs`. This allows us to communicate between components, manage slots, and work with attributes effectively using the Composition API.

Exercise

Modify the `PersonGreeting` component to have a text input that allows the user to change the name. When the button is clicked, the event should send the updated name to the parent component.

Solution

```
<template>
  <div>
    <input type="text" v-model="fullName" />
    <button @click="sendEvent">Call Heroes</button>
  </div>
</template>

<script>
import { ref } from 'vue';

export default {
  setup(props, context) {
    const fullName = ref('David Stone');

    const sendEvent = () => {
      context.emit('callHeroes', fullName.value);
    };

    return {
      sendEvent,
      fullName
    };
  }
};
</script>
```

Remember: Always experiment with the `context` object to familiarize yourself with its capabilities!

Reusability

In this section, we're diving into how to reuse functionality across components using the Composition API. Remember back when we talked about mixins? Let's refresh our memory about how those worked before we get into the Composition API.

Imagine you have two components, one that counts the number of times you click a button (`ClickCounter`) and another that counts how many times you hover over a heading (`HoverCounter`). Since both have this counter functionality, we can extract the reusable logic into a `CounterMixin` in a `mixins` folder.

```js
// mixins/CounterMixin.js
export default {
  data() {
    return {
      count: 0,
    };
  },
  methods: {
    incrementCount() {
      this.count += 1;
    },
  },
};
```

Now, in our `ClickCounter` and `HoverCounter` components, we'll use the `mixins` option to include this reusable logic:

```vue
// components/ClickCounter.vue
<template>
  <button @click="incrementCount">Click Me:
{{ count }}</button>
</template>

<script>
import CounterMixin from './mixins/CounterMixin';

export default {
  mixins: [CounterMixin],
};
</script>
```

```vue
// components/HoverCounter.vue
<template>
  <h1 @mouseover="incrementCount">Hover Me: {{ count }}</h1>
</template>

<script>
import CounterMixin from './mixins/CounterMixin';

export default {
  mixins: [CounterMixin],
};
</script>
```

In the browser, you'll see both counters working as expected. But, while mixins work, they have some drawbacks.

The biggest issue is that mixins can be conflict-prone. Since properties are merged into the component, you need to be aware of every option in the mixin to avoid naming collisions. Imagine having multiple mixins for a component—it's a recipe for confusion trying to figure out where everything is coming from!

Mixins also limit reusability. We can't pass parameters to a mixin to modify its logic, reducing its flexibility.

This is where the Composition API comes in. It lets us reuse functionality while addressing the limitations of mixins. Let's see how it works using the same counter example.

First, we'll reuse our two components but comment out the mixins options since we'll replace them with the Composition API.

Next, we create a folder called composables and inside, a file called useCounter.js. This is where we'll write our reusable counter logic.

```javascript
// composables/useCounter.js
import { ref } from 'vue';

export default function useCounter(initialCount = 0,
stepSize = 1) {
  const count = ref(initialCount);

  function incrementCount() {
    count.value += stepSize;
  }

  return { count, incrementCount };
}
```

In this composable, we use the ref function from Vue to create a reactive count variable and define an incrementCount function. Finally, we return the count and incrementCount to be used in our components.

Let's import this composable into our ClickCounter and HoverCounter components.

```html
// components/ClickCounter.vue
<template>
  <button @click="incrementCount">Click Me:
{{ count }}</button>
```

```
</template>

<script>
import useCounter from './composables/useCounter.js';

export default {
  setup() {
    const { count, incrementCount } = useCounter(100, 10);
    return { count, incrementCount };
  },
};
</script>
```

In this example, we passed in `100` and `10` as initial count and step size for our `ClickCounter` component, making the button increment by 10.

```
// components/HoverCounter.vue
<template>
  <h1 @mouseover="incrementCount">Hover Me: {{ count }}</h1>
</template>

<script>
import useCounter from './composables/useCounter.js';

export default {
  setup() {
    const { count, incrementCount } = useCounter();
    return { count, incrementCount };
  },
};
</script>
```

In the `setup` method, we call our composable `useCounter` and destructure the returned object to access the `count` and `incrementCount`. We return these so they can be used in our template.

To use `<script setup>`:

```
<script setup>
import useCounter from './composables/useCounter.js';
    const { count, incrementCount } = useCounter();
</script>
```

Now, go back to the browser. Both counters still work, but there's a key difference! We've overcome the limitations of mixins.

With composables, it's clear what functionality is being provided in our `setup` method, eliminating the confusion and potential for conflicts. The reusability is also improved. By adding parameters to our composable, we can customize the behavior, making it flexible and adaptable to different scenarios.

So, when building large applications, composables are a powerful tool for organizing and reusing code, promoting cleaner and more maintainable code. And that brings us to the end of our discussion on the Composition API.

You have mastered Vue 3! Congratulations!!!